T0339723

KAIROLOGICAL ECONOMICS

KAIROLOGICAL ECONOMICS

An Anthropocentric and
Creative Theory of
Political Economy and Management

NICOLAS LAOS

Algora Publishing
New York

Library of Congress Cataloging-in-Publication Data —

Laos, Nicolas K., 1974-
   Kairological economics: an anthropocentric and creative theory of political
economy and management / Nicolas Laos.
      p. cm.
   Includes bibliographical references and index.
      ISBN 978-0-87586-951-3 (pbk.: alk. paper) — ISBN 978-0-87586-952-0
(alk. paper) — ISBN 978-0-87586-953-7 (ebook) 1. Diplomacy. 2. Cultural
relations. 3. International relations—Philosophy. I. Title.
   JZ1305.L364 2012
   327.201—dc23
                              2012033442

Printed in the United States

TABLE OF CONTENTS

Preface

The ideas expressed in this book were shaped by my work as a political and economic consultant, by my academic research and by methodic observations of different countries and organizations. My conclusions from the previous activities are the following: (i) mainstream, 'normal' Economics and Management, as academic disciplines, are, to a large extent, fixated in obsolete ontological and epistemological assumptions; (ii) the academic disciplines of Economics and Management need to be thoroughly re-evaluated (and revised) with respect to the epistemological and ontological advances that took place in philosophy and the natural sciences in the 20th century; (iii) there is a critical yet elusive dependence of economics and policy analysis on philosophical questions; (iv) economic analysis must be focused on the relationship between the reality of the world as a tank of opportunities and the reality of consciousness as a tank of intentions, and, therefore, it must stress and investigate the submissiveness of reality to the intentionality of human consciousness. In this book, I attempt to establish a new 'school' of economic and managerial thought, which I call Kairological Economics, after the name of Kairos, the ancient Greek god of opportunity.

Fortunately, I was able to test my ideas against the critical argument of my interdisciplinary colleagues in several American and European academic institutions and of my associates in the steering committee of the "Kairological Society — Reality Restructuring Resources Ltd", an international philosophical and policy-oriented think-tank and consultancy organization. Especially my cooperation with the distinguished business and financial consultants Mr Leonidas Dimitroulias (C.E.O., Protypi Economici S.A.), Mr Theodore Chouliaras (C.E.O., Upmaritime London Ltd), Mr Theodoros Chrysis (Member of the Board, Sofia Finance AD), Mr John Moustos (Investment Banking Director, CapitalOne Investment Group) and Mr Panos Panagiotou has been a very pleasant and creative experience.

The structure of the present book is based on the research work that I conducted as a lecturer at the workshop "Charting Troubled Waters: Policy Analysis for Uncertain Times" that was organized by RAND Corporation scholars at the Hellenic American Union in Athens, Greece, in May 2012. In the context of the previous workshop, my communication with Dr Warren E. Walker, Professor of Policy Analysis at the Delft University of Technology and Operations Research scholar associated with the RAND Corporation, Dr Adnan Rahman, Principal and Director of the International Division of Cambridge Systematics and former Director of Business Development at RAND Europe, Mr Marc Leipoldt, Managing Director of Global Risk Advisory Services, Mr Dimitris Vayenas, IT expert with rich industrial experience, Dr John M. Nomikos, Director of the Research Institute for European and American Studies (RIEAS), and other people from industry, government, banking and academia has helped me to chart thoroughly and effectively the major epistemological, ontological and moral problems that determine the development of policy analysis and economic thought and to define more sharply my theses.

Nicolas Laos

Chapter 1. The Philosophical Underpinnings Of Economic Analysis And Kairicity

Economic analysis underpins and informs economic decision-making, even if there is a lengthy lag between economic analysis and its gradual absorption into economic debate. Once established as common sense, a text of economic analysis becomes incredibly powerful, because it delineates not only what is the object of knowledge but also what it is sensible to talk about or suggest. If one thinks and acts outside the framework of the dominant text of economic analysis, he risks more than simply the judgment that his recommendations are wrong; his entire moral attitude may be ridiculed or seen as dangerous just because his theoretical assumptions are deemed unrealistic. Therefore, defining common sense and, in essence, what is 'reality' and 'realistic' is the ultimate act of political power. Economic analysis does not simply explain or predict; it tells us what possibilities exist for human action and intervention; it defines both our explanatory possibilities and our moral and practical horizons. Hence, ontology and epistemology matter, and the stakes are far more considerable than at first sight seem to be the case.

One of the major goals of philosophy is to identify the relations between consciousness and external reality. The various relations that can be conceived with respect to consciousness and external reality are reducible to two general philosophical models: realism and idealism. In general, philosophical realism consists in the following thesis: since experience provides consciousness with images of a reality that seems to be external to our minds, it naturally follows that this reality is the cause that generates the set of the given partial images, and, therefore, according to the principle of causality, a mind-independent reality exists necessarily. Whereas the representatives of realism emphasize the principle of causality, the representatives of idealism emphasize the principle of identity. In other words, according to idealism, the nature of consciousness and the nature of external reality are neither totally different from each other nor opposite of each other. Idealists view the world not as something reflected in consciousness, but as an extension and a projection of consciousness out of itself and also as consciousness itself.

The social sciences in general and economics in particular are characterized by several debates between realists and idealists. Moreover, the antithesis between realism and idealism in economics and in the social sciences in general has taken various forms, which often complicate the debate between realist and idealist scholars. In the scientific field of economics, Uskali Mäki argues that taking a realist position is pragmatic insofar as he fears that rejecting realism "would result in the worst kind of complacency"[1]. Tony Lawson has defined the scope of his own realist project as follows:

> [M]y strategy has just been to seek to explain [aspects of] certain human actions, to identify their conditions of possibility. Or, more precisely, my strategy has been to explain various generalised features of experience, including human actions, and so to uncover generalised insights regarding the structure

---

1 Uskali Mäki, "Some Non-Reasons for Non-Realism in Economics", in U. Mäki (ed.), *Fact and Fiction in Economics: Realism, Models and Social Construction*, Cambridge: Cambridge University Press, 2002, p. 102.

or nature of reality. This of course, is precisely an exercise in ontology.[2]

Additionally, Lawson explains the significance of ontological questions in the scientific discipline of economics as follows:

> In identifying my project as realist I am first and foremost wanting to indicate a *conscious* and *sustained* orientation towards examining, and formulating *explicit* positions concerning the nature and structure of social reality, as well as investigating the nature and grounds of ontological (and other) presuppositions of prominent or otherwise significant or interesting contributions. And I am wanting to suggest that it is precisely this sort of *explicit concern* with questions of ontology that is (or has been) lacking in modern economics. This is an absence, indeed, that I believe contributes significantly to the discipline's current malaise. In this sense of the term, in my view, most of the projects contributing to the development of modern economics are not nearly realist enough.[3]

On the other hand, Simon Deichsel's conception of anti-realism runs as follows:

> I take anti-realism as the thesis that we should suspend judgement on the truth and truth-worthiness of our theories or avoid talking about the truth of theories altogether in order to minimize the confusions that surround this concept.[4]

Additionally, Deichsel writes:

> There are at least three reasons why I disagree with [Lawson's] position: first, we cannot know what the "real forces" are; second, [Lawson's] proposal can be turned against any form of idealisation; and third, it is doubtful whether mainstream economics is well characterised by Lawson's interpretation of the term "deductivism" at all.[5]

The traditional epistemological schools

Empiricism is the view that the only grounds for justified belief are those that rest ultimately on observation. Based on the philosophies of David Hume and John Locke, the central empiricist prem-

---

2 Tony Lawson, *Reorienting Economics*, London: Routledge, 2003, p. 33.

3 Ibid., p. 72.

4 Simon Deichsel, "Against the Pragmatic Justification for realism in Economic Methodology", *Erasmus Journal for Philosophy and Economics*, Vol. 4, 2011, pp. 23-41.

5 Ibid., p. 34.

ise is that science must be based on a phenomenalist nominalism, i.e., the notion that only statements that refer to observable phenomena are cognitively significant and that any statements that do not refer to independent atomized objects cannot be granted the status of justified knowledge[6]. According to empiricism, science can be founded on a bedrock of such objective sense data ('pure observation'), and from this bedrock can be established, by induction, the entire structure of science.

But empiricism has the following defects: (i) The epistemological warrant offered by empiricism is very narrow, because it is based on direct observation, and, therefore, it rules out any consideration of (unobservable) things, e.g. social structures, or even social facts (which, according to E. Durkheim, refer to those shared social concepts and understandings such as crime, which he argued that should be treated as 'things'). Hence, a strict empiricism actually offers a very restricted understanding of 'reality'. (ii) Empiricism does not allow us to talk about 'causes', since these are unobservable. In the context of empiricism, causation is reduced to mere correlation, and our enquiry is therefore limited to that of 'prediction' and cannot involve 'explanation'. (iii) The kind of pure unvarnished perception requested by empiricists is impossible. John Searle has pointed out that subjectivity is an essential characteristic of conscious states[7], and W.V.O. Quine has pointed out that theory is involved in all empirical observation, thus making absolute objectivism impossible[8]. Furthermore, both Immanuel Kant and Gestalt Psychology[9] have pointed out that the conscious mind plays a much more active role in perception than the one thought by empiricists.

---

6 Leszek Kolakowski, *Positivist Philosophy*, Harmondsworth: Penguin Books, 1972, p. 11–17.

7 John Searle, *The Rediscovery of the Mind*, Cambridge, Mass.: MIT Press, 1992.

8 W.V.O. Quine, "Two Dogmas of Empiricism", in W.V.O. Quine (ed.), *From a Logical Point of View*, 2nd edition, Cambridge, MA: Harvard University Press, 1961, p. 20–46.

9 Gestalt Psychology was founded by Max Wertheimer (1880–1943). Wertheimer noted that we perceive motion where there is nothing more than a rapid sequence of individual sensory events. This argument is based on observations he made with his stroboscope at the

Rationalism is based on the philosophies of René Descartes, Gottfried Wilhelm Leibniz and Baruch Spinoza, and it has been the historical counterpoint to Hume's and Locke's empiricism. Rationalism was very much influenced by the scientific revolution of Newton, Kepler and Galileo, and thus it has subscribed to the view that the kinds of mechanisms discovered by the previous natural scientists were quite different kinds of things to those which people can observe. In other words, rationalists stress that perception or observation is never sufficient on its own, and it requires logical processing. The central rationalist premise is that the sense cannot give us an understanding of the mechanisms that generate the observables we perceive and that the notion of logic, which is a property of the human intellect, can work out the relationship between observables and deduce the causal mechanisms at work. We can only gain knowledge of the world by using logic in order to process-explain what we observe or experience. This notion of rationality, with mathematics as the exemplar, was based on a foundation of certain truth, which for Descartes was an intuitive truth known by all minds; thus he declared "cogito ergo sum" (I think, therefore I am): reflective minds could doubt everything, except they could not doubt that they were thinking, and this provides the basis for secure knowledge about the world.

But rationalism has the following defects: (i) There is more than one kind of rationality, if, in Cartesian spirit, we take it to mean a deductive system based on intuitive axioms. Different individuals might claim that their intuitions were different from those of others. For instance, Descartes claimed that Euclidean geometry was absolute, being based on definitive axioms, but Riemann, Lobachevsky

---

Frankfurt train station and on additional observations he made in his laboratory when he experimented with lights flashing in rapid succession (like the Christmas lights that appear to course around the tree, or the fancy neon signs in Las Vegas that seem to move). Wertheimer called this effect "apparent motion", and it is actually the basic principle of motion pictures. According to Wertheimer, apparent motion proves that people don't respond to isolated segments of sensation but to the whole (*Gestalt*) of the situation. See: Wolfgang Köhler, *Gestalt Psychology*, New York: Liveright, 1992.

and other mathematicians have created non-Euclidean geometries, based on different intuitive axioms. Moreover, N.A. Vasiliev, Jan Łukasiewicz, Hans Reichenbach, A.H.S. Korzybski, Lotfi Zadeh, R.A. Wilson and other logicians have created various non-Aristotelian logics, based on different intuitive axioms. (ii) Man relates to beings and things in the world through significances that he assigns to them[10], and, therefore, the fundamental significations (i.e., the values) that underpin human action must explicitly find their position in every meaningful discussion about social systems.

Pragmatism is based on the philosophies of William James, Charles Pierce and John Dewey, and it attempts to combine the rationalist thesis that the mind is always active in interpreting experience and observation with the empiricist thesis that revisions in our beliefs are to be made as a result of experience[11]. According to pragmatism, theories are underdetermined by the evidence, and, therefore, scientists have to choose between a number of theories that may all be compatible with the available evidence. Hence, as William James has put it, truth is "only the expedient in the way of belief", meaning that we need to adjust our ideas as to what is true as experience unfolds. Pragmatism, then, defines what is true as what is most useful in the way of belief (a utilitarian epistemology).

However, pragmatism is ultimately self-defeating. Even though pragmatism appears to reflect a dynamic attitude toward reality and epistemology and to be a progressive epistemological stance, it is deeply conservative and assigns a deeply pathetic role to human consciousness. By stressing the adaptation of our ideas to an unfolding experience, pragmatists ignore the dynamic continuity between the reality of the world and the reality of consciousness, a dynamic continuity that allows conscious beings to impose their intentionality on reality, instead of merely adapting to a reality that

---

10 Ernst Cassirer, *The Philosophy of Symbolic Forms*, Volume One: Language, Volume Two: Mythical Thought, trans. R. Manheim, New Haven: Yale University Press, 1955.

11 For a general introduction to pragmatism, see for instance: C.J. Misak (ed.), *Pragmatism*, Calgary: University of Calgary Press, 1999.

is external to their consciousness. Conscious beings are not merely obliged to look for methods of adaptation to reality, but they can utilize and restructure reality according to their intentionality.

Contemporary epistemological debates

Scientific realism: it is based on the philosophies of Roy Bhaskar[12] and Rom Harré[13]. The central premise of scientific realism is that it makes sense to talk of a world outside of experience. Thus, scientific realism is primarily concerned with the uncovering of the structures and things of an objective scientific cosmos. Scientific realism treats theoretical concepts such as electrons or sets in the same way as so-called 'facts', and, therefore, it argues that the empiricist conception of the role of theories (as heuristic) is wrong. Bhaskar distinguishes among the real, the actual and the empirical: the first refers to what entities and mechanisms make up the world, the second to events, and the third to that which we experience. According to Bhaskar, empiricism makes the mistake of looking at the third of these as a way of explaining the other two so that it reduces ontological questions to epistemological questions. Furthermore, Bhaskar rejects rationalism, too, by arguing that it too reduces ontology to epistemology by its reliance on theoretically necessary conceptual truths to explain the world. In contrast to empiricism and rationalism, realist science is an attempt to describe and explain structures and processes of the world that exist independently of human consciousness.

But many of the arguments of scientific realism have been falsified by recent advances in science, especially in the context of quantum theory and cybernetics. Niels Bohr, who made foundational contributions to understanding atomic structure and quantum mechanics, is reported to have said to Werner Heisenberg, who was another great pioneer of quantum physics: in the field of atomic and sub-atomic physics, "language can be used only as in poetry", since, like poets, physicists are not concerned so much with the descrip-

---

12 Roy Bhaskar, *A Realist Theory of Science*, Brighton: Harvester, 1978.
13 Rom Harré, *Varieties of Realism*, Oxford: Blackwell, 1986.

tion of facts as with the creation of images[14]. Moreover, in the same spirit, Alfred Whitehead, who co-authored the epochal *Principia Mathematica* with B. Russell, has argued that nature is always in a state of becoming and that the reality of the natural world is the natural becoming itself[15].

Within the framework of cybernetics, epistemologists focus on the observer in addition to what is observed. Lynn Segal[16] and Ernst von Glasersfeld[17] have explained that, according to modern cybernetics, scientific laws should not be considered as discoveries, as one, for instance, might discover an island in an ocean, but they should be considered as inventions by which scientists explain regularities in their experiences. Persons interact with reality, and hence consciousness constructs and reconstructs reality.

Finally, the most catalytic argument against scientific realism is the following: if the structure of the world were totally distinct from the structure of consciousness, then the latter could not gain even partial knowledge of the first.

Phenomenology, Structuralism and Hermeneutics: For Edmund Husserl[18], phenomenology is a method according to which the researcher focuses on the essential structures that allow the objects that are taken for granted in the "natural attitude" (which is characteristic of both our everyday life and ordinary science) to "constitute themselves" in consciousness. Phenomenology is characterized by subjectivism in the sense that phenomenological inquiries are initially directed, in Cartesian fashion, toward consciousness and its presentations. On the other hand, phenomenology is not characterized

---

14 Quoted in Jacob Bronowski, *The Ascent of Man*, Boston: Little, 1974, p. 340.
15 Alfred Whitehead, *Science and the Modern World*, New York: Macmillan, 1944, p. 106.
16 Lynn Segal, *The Dream of Reality*, New York: Norton, 1986.
17 Ernst von Glasersfeld, *The Construction of Knowledge*, Salinas, CA: Intersystems, 1987.
18 See: Herbert Spiegelberg, *The Phenomenological Movement*, 3rd revised and enlarged edition, The Hague: Nijhoff, 1982; Elisabeth Ströker, *Husserl's Transcendental Phenomenology*, Stanford: Stanford University Press, 1993.

by any psychological or mentalistic forms of subjectivism, since the subject-matter of phenomenology is not the realm of psychological ideas affirmed by empiricism but rather the ideal meanings and universal relations with which consciousness is confronted in its experience.

The phenomenological method comes from a position prior to reflexive thought, called pre-reflexive thought, which consists of a turn to the very things. At that moment, the phenomenologist holds a phenomenological stance that enables him to keep himself open enough to live that experience in its wholeness, preventing any judgment from interfering with his openness to the description. The phenomenologist is not concerned with the particular elements of the object under investigation, but with the given object's ideal essence which is hidden by and shines through the particulars. Husserl used the term "epoché" (suspension of judgment) to refer to the purification of experience of its factuality.

In his preface to *Ideas Pertaining to a Pure Phenomenology — First Book: General Introduction to a Pure Phenomenology*, Husserl argues that phenomenology, like mathematics, is "the science of pure possibilities" which "must everywhere precede the science of real facts." By bracketing factuality, phenomenology exerted important influence on existentialism, and, in fact, it became the method of existentialism[19], which is based on the thesis that consciousness attributes meaning to the reality of the world. In contrast to Aristotle's philosophy — which assigns primary significance to the essence of things (namely, to the attribute or set of attributes that make an object what it fundamentally is, and which it has by necessity, and without which it loses its identity) — the philosophers of existence, such as S.A. Kierkegaard, Martin Heidegger and J.-P. Sartre, argue that what is ontologically significant is not the essence of being but the presence of being, i.e., its existence.

The next major step in the development of the phenomenological method took place when it was applied in the investigation of

---

19 See: Haim Gordon, *Dictionary of Existentialism*, New York: Greenwood Press, 1999; Thomas Flynn, *Existentialism: A Very Short Introduction*, Oxford: Oxford University Press, 2006.

those elements of reality whose knowledge is prior to the knowledge of the essence of reality, i.e., when it was applied in the investigation of the elements that constitute the structure of reality. By the term 'structure', we mean an intimate reality that is organized and re-organized by itself and that is determined by its own order, which also constitutes the core of the given structure. The method of structuralism is the final stage of phenomenology's attempt to cope with the problems that emerge from the philosophical investigation of the intimate meaning of reality. Additionally, structuralism corroborates Gaston Bachelard's argument that there is a dynamic continuity between knowing consciousness and known object[20].

Closely related to the project of investigating the intimate meaning of reality is Gadamer's method of hermeneutics. Its central premise is anti-naturalist in that it does not see the social world as in any sense amenable to the empiricist and especially the positivist epistemology. Hermeneutics, having developed out of textual analysis, emphasizes the difference between the analysis of nature ('explanation') and the analysis of the mind ('understanding'). Karl Jaspers[21] defines the scientific analysis of "objective causal connections" as "explaining" ("Erklären"), whereas he designates the "understanding of psychic events 'from within'" as "understanding" ("Verstehen"). In this way, Jaspers' thought opened the philosophical path to Gadamer's hermeneutics.

According to hermeneutics, we can only understand the world by our being caught up in a system of significance. Persons analyze and act within what Gadamer[22] refers to as an "horizon", by which he means their beliefs, preconceptions and in general their embeddedness in the particular history and culture that shaped them. Thus, from the viewpoint of hermeneutics, the notions of truth and reason are consequences of man's embeddedness in systems

---

20 See: Mary Tiles, *Bachelard: Science and Objectivity*, Cambridge: Cambridge University Press, 1984.

21 See: P.A. Schilpp (ed.), *The Philosophy of Karl Jaspers*, New York: Tudor Publishing Company, 1957.

22 H.-G. Gadamer, *Truth and Method*, London: Sheed and Ward, 1975.

of significance (value systems). Epistemology, hence, can never be something prior to or independent of culture and has to be seen as secondary to ontology.

Critical Theory: it has developed out the work of the Frankfurt School in the inter-war years[23], and its most influential thinker has been Jürgen Habermas. Habermas has put forward the thesis that there are three types of knowledge[24]: empirical-analytical (the natural sciences), historical-hermeneutic (concerned with meaning and understanding), and critical sciences (concerned with emancipation). According to Habermas, each of these types of knowledge has its own set of "cognitive interests", respectively: those of a technical interest in control and prediction, a practical interest in understanding, and an emancipatory interest in enhancing freedom. From the viewpoint of the Critical School, there can be so such thing as true (interest-free) empirical statements (e.g., in the realm of the natural sciences independent of the knowledge-constitutive interest in control and prediction).

However, in the late 1960s, Habermas moved away from the above-mentioned rather restricted notion of knowledge-constitutive interests toward the development of what he calls a theory of communicative action[25]. Thus, his epistemology is based on the notion of discourse ethics or universal pragmatics, according to which knowledge emerges out of a consensus theory of truth. Central to his epistemology is his idea of an 'ideal speech situation', which he sees as implicit in the act of communication and as rationally entailing moral and normative commitments. The 'ideal speech situation'[26] is based on the notion that acts of communication necessarily presuppose that statements are: (i) comprehensible, (ii) true, (iii) right

---

23 David Held, *Introduction to Critical Theory*, Berkeley, CA: University of California Press, 1980.

24 Jürgen Habermas, *Knowledge and Human Interests*, Cambridge: Polity, 1987 (first published 1968).

25 Jürgen Habermas, *The Theory of Communicative Action, Vol. 2: The Critique of Functionalist Reason*, Cambridge: Polity, 1987.

26 See: William Outhwaite, *Habermas: A Critical Introduction*, Cambridge: Polity, 1994, p. 40.

and (iv) sincere. Habermas is aware that the ideal speech situation is something that is not commonly found in communicative actions, but he believes that we could in principle reach a consensus on the validity of the previous four claims, and that this consensus would be achieved if we envisaged a situation in which coercive power and distortion were removed from communication so that the "force of the better argument prevails"[27]. Hence, Habermas, following Kantianism, seeks to avoid the simple objectivism of positivism whilst at the same time refusing to endorse the kind of relativism implicit in traditional hermeneutics.

Post-modernism seeks the overthrow of virtually all preceding positions of epistemology, and it is strongly influenced by the philosophy of Friedrich Nietzsche. Michel Foucault, one of the most influential post-modern scholars, argues that "nothing in man — not even his body — is sufficiently stable to serve as the basis for self-recognition or for understanding other men" ;[28] therefore, there is no escape from the functioning of power and contingency, and struggle is always necessary to avoid domination.

Is the will for truth a truth, or is it simply another name for the will for power (and authority)? "What in us really wants 'truth'?" Nietzsche's answer is the will for power. This is Foucault's epistemological thesis, too. Moreover, following this Nietzschean epistemological argument, Jacques Derrida, one of most influential post-modernists, developed the theory of deconstruction, according to which texts collapse under their own weight once it is demonstrated that their 'truth content' is merely the "mobile army of metaphors" identified by Nietzsche[29].

From the viewpoint of Nietzsche's approach to the will for power, a false judgment can be seen as an expression of creativity, and, hence, it can be interpreted as a consequence of a dynamic attitude to life. But, when philosophy recognizes untruth as a condition of

---

27 Ibid., p. 40.
28 Michel Foucault, *Language, Counter-Memory, Practice*, ed. D.F. Bouchard, Ithaca, NY: Cornell University Press, 1977, p. 153.
29 See: Christopher Norris, *Derrida*, London: Fontana, 1987

life and therefore it moves beyond every distinction between good and evil, identifying will as such with truth, then it is necessarily indifferent as to whether an untrue judgment underpins injustice and violence. In other words, Nietzsche respects creativity as such, without any further qualifications. But, in this way, contrary to the classical Greek philosophers' approach to creativity, Nietzsche's approach to creativity is unable to provide a solid foundation of life[30].

As I have pointed out in my book *Foundations of Cultural Diplomacy*, Nietzsche argues that philosophers are dishonest because they pretend that their thoughts echo objective reality, whereas, for Nietzsche, what they really do is to reduce their prejudices, their ideas, to "the truth"[31]. In reality, Nietzsche contends, philosophers defend judgments that are equivalent to advocates' tricks or their own hearts' desires but they present them in abstract forms and by means of arguments which they have articulated after (not before) the original conception of their ideas. It is useful to mention that this Nietzschean thesis underpins Richard Rorty's post-modern approach to epistemology, according to which philosophers should give up on the idea that our knowledge 'mirrors' nature and instead adopt a pragmatic theory of truth, which is compatible with Rorty's self-description as a "postmodern bourgeois liberal"[32]. However, as I have argued in my previous book, Nietzsche makes a mistake: the validity of truth does not depend on its genealogy but on its logic, its consistence, and the logic of truth depends on the fact that it can harmoniously unite a multitude of data toward a specific perspective. Therefore, philosophers (at least when they do not have the arrogance of Hegel to declare that their philosophies mark the end of the history of philosophy) are not as dishonest as Nietzsche contends.

---

30 See: Nicolas Laos, *Foundations of Cultural Diplomacy: Politics Among Cultures and the Moral Autonomy of Man*, New York: Algora Publishing, 2011, Section 2.8.

31 Ibid.

32 Richard Rorty, *Objectivity, Relativism and Truth: Philosophical Papers*, Vol. I, Cambridge: Cambridge University Press, 1991, p. 197-202.

Kairos: beyond realism and idealism

'Kairos' means the 'opportune moment'. The concept of kairos can be traced back to the ancient Greek philosophy and Pantheon. In particular, in the ancient Greek mythology, the notion of kairos was divinized, and Kairos was a son of Zeus. For instance, Aesop (*Fables* 536, from *Phaedrus* 5:8) writes: "Running swiftly, balancing on the razor's edge, bald but with a lock of hair on his forehead, he wears no clothes; if you grasp him from the front, you might be able to hold him, but once he has moved on not even Jupiter [Zeus] himself can pull him back: this is a symbol of Tempus [Kairos] (Opportunity), the brief moment in which things are possible." The famous Greek travelogue writer Pausanias, in his *Description of Greece*, 5.14.9 (trans. W.H.S. Jones), writes about Kairos: "Quite close to the entrance to the stadium [at Olympia] are two altars; one they call the altar of Hermes of the Games, the other the altar of Kairos (Opportunity). I know that a hymn to Kairos is one of the poems of Ion of Khios [5th century BC poet]; in the hymn Kairos is made out to be the youngest child of Zeus." Moreover, Callistratus (Greek rhetorician who flourished in the 3rd/ 4th century AD), in his *Descriptions* 6 (trans. by A. Fairbanks), wrote about Kairos: "On the statue of Kairos (Opportunity) at Sikyon. I desire to set before you in words the creation of Lysippos [4th century BC sculptor] also, the most beautiful of statues, which the artist wrought and set up for the Sikyonians to look upon. Kairos (Opportunity) was represented in a statue of bronze...but a man who was skilled in the arts and who, with a deeper perception of art, knew how to track down the marvels of craftsmen, applied reasoning to the artist's creation, explaining the significance of Kairos (Opportunity) as faithfully portrayed in the statue: the wings on his feet, he told us, suggested his swiftness, and that, borne by the seasons, he goes rolling on through all eternity; and as to his youthful beauty, that beauty is always opportune and that Kairos (Opportunity) is the only artificer of beauty, whereas that of which the beauty has withered has no part in the nature of Kairos (Opportunity); he also explained that the lock of hair on his forehead indicated that while he is easy to catch as he approaches, yet, when he has passed by, the moment of action has likewise expired, and that, if opportunity (kairos) is neglected, it cannot be recovered."

The concepts of kairos and kairicity[33] do not merely refer to the sense of timing, but they signify something much more important than that. They signify that, even though the reality of the world is not a projection of human consciousness, it can, nevertheless, under certain conditions, be utilized and restructured by the intentionality of human consciousness. Philosophical realism sees 'Kairos' as if he were totally bald, i.e., it fails to notice and grab the lock of hair that exists on Kairos' forehead, whereas idealism sees Kairos as if he had hair on the back of his head, too, i.e., it fails to understand that Kairos cannot be arbitrarily manipulated. A kairic consciousness, contra realism and idealism, is aware that the reality of the world and the reality of consciousness are not one, but they are united with each other. Therefore, a kairic consciousness recognizes and respects the 'otherness' of the reality of the world, but simultaneously it acts in order to impose its intentionality on the reality of the world. Moreover, Hunter W. Stephenson[34] has drawn an analogy between kairos and archery, and he argues that kairos represents the moment in which one may fire an arrow with sufficient force to penetrate the target.

The philosophical method that invokes the kairicity of consciousness is derived from the synthesis between structuralism and hermeneutics. On the basis of the kairicity of consciousness, we can interpret both ontological reality and the intentionality of consciousness, which imposes its own structures on ontological reality in order to utilize ontological reality. As a criterion of reality and action, kairicity stems from consciousness, but, since it is not intended to offer philosophical 'legitimacy' to arbitrary idealistic action, it is activated only when it is possible to be applied on objective real-

---

33 In my book *The Rediscovery of Western Esotericism* (Northampton, UK: White Crane Publishing, 2012), I elucidate the significance of kairicity in the fields of ontology, epistemology and ethics.

34 H.W. Stephenson, *Forecasting Opportunity: Kairos, Production and Writing,* Lanham, Maryland: University Press of America, 2005.

ity. Additionally, the method of kairicity is based on the ontological position that objective reality is activated for consciousness when consciousness assigns meaning and significance to objective reality. Even though reality is multidimensional, it becomes significant for consciousness only when it becomes updated in relation to the intentionality of consciousness. Therefore, the knowledge of reality that is based on the method of kairicity is in agreement with both the nature of consciousness and the nature of reality.

The method of kairicity consists in the following four-fold dialectic, which I shall henceforth call the *dialectic of kairicity*: (i) first, consciousness imagines an ideal state of the world and intends to intervene in the reality of the world in order to transcend the established state of the world and improve the conditions under which existence is confirmed; (ii) second, consciousness endorses the Aristotelian doctrine of the mean and intends to act on the reality of the world in such a manner that it will not cause uncontrolled turbulence, which could ultimately put the continuity of existence in danger; (iii) when the turbulence that is caused by the action of consciousness on the world tends to become chaotic, consciousness tries to reduce the negative consequences of its action by taking new action that balances its previous action, i.e., it follows a policy of risk management that averts both the total elimination of the previous state of the world and the emergence of a totally unknown new order of things; (iv) fourth, during its action on the reality of the world, consciousness intends to create the necessary conditions that will allow consciousness to continue acting on the reality of the world in the future. Whenever a conscious being follows the previous four-fold dialectic, we say that it is characterized by kairicity, or that it acts kairically.

If the structure of the world were totally distinct from the structure of consciousness, then the latter would be unable to gain even partial knowledge of the reality of the world (it could only know itself). If the reality of the world were merely a projection of human consciousness, i.e., if the reality of the world were identified with the contents of human consciousness, then consciousness would not try so hard to know the world, and the knowledge of the world would be identified with the knowledge of the self. Thus, neither realism nor idealism can stand as a general theory of reality. Kairicity implies that there is a dynamic continuity between the reality of the world and the reality of consciousness. Therefore, economic analysis should be focused on the analysis of the relationship between the reality of the world as a tank of opportunities and the reality of consciousness as a tank of intentions. This is the essence of what I call kairological economics.

A kairic approach to policy analysis[35]

These are ten definitions of kairological policy analysis:

1. A process for organizing information about the reality of the world as a tank of opportunities and about the reality of the actors' consciousness as a tank of intentions, in order to help decision-making on the basis of the dialectic of kairicity.

2. The examination of questions related to the policy-making process, conducted with the intention to achieve a dialectical transcendence of the antithesis between realism and idealism and hence to affect the policy-making process.

3. Analysis that generates information in such a way as to improve the basis for policy-makers to exercise the kairicity of their consciousness.

4. Analysis that assists policy-makers in understanding complex problems of policy choice in an environment characterized by a dialectical relationship between necessity and freedom.

5. Analysis that assists policy-makers to develop, understand, select and implement what should be done in an environment characterized by a dialectical relationship between necessity and freedom in order to change people's existential conditions according to their intentionality — and what consequences to evaluate.

---

35 In this section, based on the above-mentioned method of kairicity, I amend definitions of policy analysis that are contained in Adnan Rahman's research paper "Policy Analysis for Uncertain Times", which he presented at a workshop on policy analysis that took place at the Hellenic American Union, Athens, Greece, in May 2012.

6. The systematic examination and comparison of alternative future policies by applying the method of kairicity.

7. The application of the method of kairicity in order to solve problems an organization is called upon to do something about.

8. Analysis that assists policy-makers to ameliorate the problems and manage the policy issues they face by applying the method of kairicity, utilizing scientific and technological advances and considering the larger contexts and uncertainties that inevitably attend such problems.

9. Keeping policy-makers' consciousness constantly alert, warning them of the risks of leaving policy issues to the hands of any kind of 'automatic pilot' and preventing them from confusing momentum with purpose.

10. Smashing the illusion that policy-makers can avoid recourse to personal judgment and responsibility as the final detriment of policy and attempting to bring about an environment that constantly produces new and not yet imagined types of performance (instead of simply performing the familiar).

Chapter 2. Economic Laws

In the philosophy of science, by the term 'law' we mean a proposition that establishes a relation between variables, variables being concepts that can take different values. The concept of a 'natural law' has been central to our understanding of the natural sciences. The history of modern political economy can be traced back to physiocracy, which was the first methodical attempt to explain economic behavior in similar ways to natural (that is, inanimate) behavior. Physiocracy was particularly dominated by François Quesnay (1694–1774) and Anne-Robert-Jacques Turgot (1727–1781). According to the physiocrats, there was a 'natural order' that allowed human beings to live together. Within the framework of the physiocrats' political economy, the human being is merged with the natural world, so that it reduces to merely a particular consequence of the operation of natural laws. Paul Samuelson and William D. Nordhaus write about physiocracy:

> A remarkable depiction of the economy as a circular flow, still used in today's texts...was made by Quesnay, Louis XIV's court physician. He stressed that the different elements of the econo-

my are as integrally tied together as are the blood vessels of the body.[36]

The founder of the so-called classical economics is Adam Smith (1723–1790). The thought of the physiocrats and other 18th century economists as well as the mentality of industrialism converge in the publication by Adam Smith of *The Wealth of Nations* in 1776, which "marks the birthdate of modern economics"[37]. In this book, Adam Smith, analyzed the price system, the distribution of income and various theories of wages, and he performed an empirical study of inflation. However, his most important contribution to economic analysis is his attempt to place the economic rationale of the physiocrats within a scientifically rigorous analytical setting by arguing that the market mechanism is a self-regulating 'natural' order and that the price system organizes the behavior of people in an automatic fashion.

In the half century after *The Wealth of Nations* appeared, the law of diminishing returns was formulated by Thomas Malthus (1766–1834) and David Ricardo (1722–1823). Campbell McConnel has explained the law of diminishing returns as follows:

> Imagine an economy whose property resources (land and real capital) are absolutely fixed. In particular, visualize a primitive, underdeveloped economy whose stock of capital goods is negligible and whose supply of arable land is fixed. Assume, too, that technology...is fixed; this means that the *quality* of capital and labor are both given. Assuming its population is growing, the simple agrarian society is concerned primarily with adding labor to a fixed amount of land and a few rudimentary farm tools to produce the food and fiber needed by its population...The law of diminishing returns indicates that *as successive equal increments of one resource (labor, in this case) are added to a fixed resource (land and property), beyond some point the resulting increases in total output will diminish in size.*[38]

Furthermore, Samuelson and Nordhaus have made the following comment about the law of diminishing returns:

---

36 P.A. Samuelson and W.D. Nordhaus, *Economics*, 14th edition, New York: McGraw-Hill, 1992, p. 376.

37 Ibid., p. 376.

38 C.R. McConnel, *Economics*, 5th edition, New York: McGraw-Hill, 1972, pp. 345-346.

> [I]ronically, just as the Industrial Revolution in the West was offsetting the dire workings of that dismal law, the Reverend T.R. Malthus...enunciated the *iron law of wages*, holding that population growth will inevitably drive workers' wages down to subsistence level.[39]

For Ricardo (from whose thinking neoclassical and in general modern economics are derived), given that the total social product is limited by diminishing returns, "what was gained by one social class had to be taken away from another one"[40]. In the 19th century, the reactions of both capitalists and socialists to Ricardo's thought was positive, for different reasons though:

> No wonder the capitalists like Ricardo. They could find quotations in his work to prove that trade unions and reforms can do little for the masses. No wonder the socialists liked Ricardo. They found in him a proof that capitalism would have to be destroyed if workers were to win their rightful share of national output.[41]

Following the intellectual legacy of Ricardo, in the 1870s, W. Stanley Jevons (1835–1882) in England, Carl Menger (1840–1921) in Austria, and Léon Walras (1834–1910) in Switzerland, working independently from each other, founded modern ('neoclassical') economics "by devising an analysis that could synthesize both demand elements and cost elements"[42]. Moreover, Walras devised a method of analyzing the economy as a whole. In particular, Walras started from the following definitions: (i) A market for a particular commodity is in equilibrium if, at the current price of the commodity, the quantity of the commodity demanded by potential buyers equals the quantity supplied by potential sellers. (ii) An economy is in general equilibrium if the markets for all goods and services are simultaneously in equilibrium. (iii) Excess demand refers to a situation in which a market is not in equilibrium at a specific price because the quantity of the commodity demanded by potential buyers exceeds the quantity supplied by potential sellers at that specific price. Then he formulated the following law, known as Walras's

---

39 Samuelson and Nordhaus *Economics*, p. 377.
40 Ibid., p. 377.
41 Ibid., p. 377.
42 Ibid., p. 378.

law: the existence of excess supply in one market must be matched by excess demand in another market, and, thus, finally, it balances out.

The physiocrats, the classical economists, and the neoclassical economists follow a positivist epistemology, which has been summarized by J.E. Cairnes as follows:

> Political Economy is a science in the same sense in which Astronomy, Dynamics, Chemistry, Physiology are sciences. Its subject-matter is different; it deals with the phenomena of wealth, while they deal with the phenomena of the physical universe; but its methods, its aims, the character of its conclusions, are the same as theirs. What Astronomy does for the phenomena of the heavenly bodies; what Dynamics does for the phenomena of motion; what Chemistry does for the phenomena of chemical combination; what Physiology does for the phenomena of the functions of organic life, that Political Economy does for the phenomena of wealth: it expounds the laws according to which these phenomena co-exist with or succeed each other; that is to say, it expounds the laws of the phenomena of wealth.[43]

In general, modern economics[44] is dominated by the argument that there are economic laws and that the primary aim of economics is the discovery of those laws. Thus, in the light of the arguments that I put forward in Chapter 1, the dominant theories of modern economics are fixated in philosophical realism and Newtonian mechanics. Alexander Woodcock and Monte Davis have pointed out that, even in the context of natural sciences, "Newton's triumph was not an explanation of anything", and that "it is possible to see the shapes of processes within the traditional framework, but only for a certain class of processes — those involving continuous change".[45] "Many processes", Woodcock and Davis continue, "yield graphs with ostensibly ill-behaved curves...The planets travel in stately Newtonian paths, but meanwhile winds wrap themselves

43 J.E. Cairnes, *The Character and Logical Method of Political Economy*, London: Macmillan, 1888, p. 35.
44 See: Harold Kincaid, *Philosophical Foundations of the Social Sciences: Analyzing Controversies in Social Research*, Cambridge: Cambridge University Press, 1996; Alexander Rosenberg, *Microeconomic Laws: A Philosophical Analysis*, Pittsburgh: University of Pittsburgh Press, 1976.
45 Alexander Woodcock and Monte Davis, *Catastrophe Theory*, London: Penguin Books, 1991, pp. 10, 14

into hurricanes, chickens alternate with eggs, and we change our minds".[46] Thus, Woodcock and Davis observe that "the twentieth century has taught us that the universe is a queerer place than we imagined, perhaps (in J.B.S. Haldane's words) queerer than we *can* imagine",[47] and that "much of reality is not so obliging".[48]

Kairology — namely, the methodical study of the kairicity of consciousness, which I delineated in Chapter 1 — implies that there is a dynamic continuity between the structure of consciousness and the structure of the world, a dynamic continuity that allows consciousness to reconstruct and utilize economic reality. Furthermore, from the viewpoint of kairology, which I defend in this book, the scientific world conception is not a 'world' more than it is a 'conception'.

Science is a form of consciousness erection, in the sense that it aims at creating theories that help consciousness to approach reality (both the reality of consciousness and the reality of the world). During the process of scientific creation, consciousness passes through three stages[49]: (i) the first stage consists in an intuitive, general comprehension of its object; (ii) the second stage consists in an analytical discernment of the constituent elements of the given object in order to be systematically investigated; (iii) the third stage consists in a synthetic reassemblage of the previous elements, so that consciousness can arrive at the final interpretation of its scientific object as a whole.

In the light of the dialectic of kairicity, which I have defined in Chapter 1, it follows that analysis and synthesis constitute an important dual tool by means of which consciousness reconstructs and utilizes reality. From this perspective, reality is not merely an object whose partial expressions are statically conceived by scientific minds; instead, reality is a goal toward which scientific consciousness is dynamically oriented, and also scientific con-

---

46 Ibid., p. 14.

47 Ibid., p. 11.

48 Ibid., p. 14.

49 For an extensive analysis of these issues, see: Martin Curd and J.A. Cover, *Philosophy of Science: The Central Issues*, New York: W.W. Norton & Co., 1998.

sciousness pursues the identification of reality with scientific consciousness itself. In other words, by completing its program, scientific consciousness tends to annihilate the distance that originally separated it from its object. Hence, the completion of the previous scientific process marks the cancellation of the original scientific object and its transformation into a mental creation, and, at a next stage, the previous scientific process leads to the objectivation of the theory that follows from the given scientific process. Therefore, the construction of a scientific theory is experienced as a scientific-consciousness erection.

At this point, we must explain the difference between social science and natural science. As Michael Nicholson has pointed out, "at the most general level a social science is the study of human beings in a social context"[50], and "international relations is just one of those contexts and we would expect the same problems and probabilities to be involved in it as with any other social science"[51]. Therefore, according to Nicholson, "the central question is, to what extent can these phenomena be described by the same sort of procedures as natural phenomena, such as planets or genes, and are the differences, which clearly exit, of such a nature as to preclude their analysis by the same sorts of methods?"[52]

To answer the previous question, we must explain the difference between the evolution of the physical world and history. The evolution of the physical world has undergone and continues undergoing several crises. Prigogine and Stengers have emphasized the dynamic character of the world of nature: "Our universe has a pluralistic, complex character. Structures may disappear, but also they may appear. Some processes are, as far as we know, well described by deterministic equations, but other involve probabilistic processes".[53] However, none of the crises of the physical world can be considered as an object of history or of social-scientific research

50 Michael Nicholson, *Causes and Consequences in International Relations: A Conceptual Study*, London: Pinter, 1996, p. 54.

51 Ibid., p. 54.

52 Ibid., p. 54.

53 Ilya Prigogine and Isabelle Stengers, *Order Out of Chaos: Man's New Dialogue with Nature*, New York: Bantam, 1984, p. 9.

unless it has affected a human society. In order for an event to be considered as 'historical', it must involve man, because history is an exclusively human creation and an exclusive characteristic of human life. From the perspective of kairology, history is the fullest expression of man's potential, and therefore it can be identified with the evolution of the human being.

From the previous viewpoint, there is a fundamental asymmetry between physical (or astronomical) time and historical time, and, therefore, there is a fundamental asymmetry between natural science and social science. Whereas physical time is, more or less, uniform, historical time is subject to structural changes. Moreover, physical time obeys its own entropy, which means that it flows in a precise and unalterable (irreversible) direction toward a precise but unknown aim.[54] On the other hand, historical time is not characterized by any entropy, because it is a free outcome of the action of human consciousness, and, therefore, it is subject only to the laws imposed upon it by the intentionality of human consciousness through the ages. Hence, the process of history functions according to man's kairic action. In other words, the process of history combines alternatively causality and freedom, progression and regression, recurrence and uniqueness.

Because we can find causality and recurrence in history, many social scientists — especially those who follow the positivist-empiricist tradition — are led to "the notion that we can identify certain sorts of situations as the 'same', or at least 'the same' in some crucial and relevant aspects",[55] and, therefore, they argue that "generalization is possible" and "we can move on to formulating deductive theories of social behavior in the standard scientific way and devise a social science of behavior in this mode".[56] On the other hand, because we can find freedom and uniqueness in history, idealists, like Peter Winch[57]

---

54 Ibid.

55 Nicholson, *Causes and Consequences in International Relations*, p. 62.

56 Ibid., p. 66.

57 According to Winch, "social relations fall into the same logical category as do relations between ideas", and, therefore, "social relations must be an equally unsuitable subject for generalizations and theories of scien-

and post-modernists, like Michel Foucault[58], Jacques Derrida[59] and Richard Rorty[60], "are averse to causal analyses of the sort practised in behavioral political science"[61] and argue that "there are no social events but multiplicities of events — perhaps as many as there are people who have experience of the event either directly, as observers or by report"[62]. All the previous views are partial approaches to reality, and, therefore, they give only a fragmented knowledge of reality. For, according to the dialectic of kairicity, history is characterized by a dynamic, dialectical relation between causality and freedom, progression and regression, recurrence and uniqueness. Therefore, neither positivism-empiricism nor idealism-postmodernism can stand as a general epistemological theory. Positivism-empiricism is philosophically justified due to the existence of causality and recurrence in history, but it cannot account for freedom and uniqueness in history.

---

tific sort to be formulated about them" (Peter Winch, *The Idea of a Social Science and Its Relation to Philosophy*, London: Routledge, 1990).

58 Foucault argues that the development of scholarly disciplines is determined by power relations and is not a neutral result of scholarly enquiry. As a result, Foucault does not ask for a correspondence theory of truth, but he construes truth as a tool for resisting power (Michel Foucault, "Nietzsche, Genealogy, History", in P. Rabinow (ed.), *The Foucault Reader*, Harmondsworth, Peregrine Books, 1986, pp. 76–100).

59 Derrida expresses his anti-foundationalist epistemology through deconstructions involving a reading of a text where the author fails to produce the conclusions he intends (Jacques Derrida, *Of Grammatology*, trans. and ed. G. Spivak, Baltimore, MD: Johns Hopkins University Press, 1976). Thus, Derrida "refuses to see the knower as a given and instead as merely one more construction of language and culture", so that "the knower is always caught up in a language and mode of thinking which, far from interpreting a world, instead constructs it" (Steve Smith, "Positivism and Beyond", in S. Smith, K. Booth and M. Zalewski (eds), *International Theory: Positivism and Beyond*, Cambridge: Cambridge University Press, 1996, p. 30).

60 The task undertaken by Rorty consists in the deconstruction of analytical philosophy, and thus he proposes that philosophers give up on the idea that our knowledge 'mirrors' nature and instead adopt a pragmatic theory of truth which is compatible with his self-description as a "postmodern bourgeois liberal" (Rorty, *Objectivity, Relativism and Truth*, Vol. I, p. 197-202).

61 Nicholson, *Causes and Consequences in International Relations*, p. 112.

62 Ibid., p. 112.

Idealists and postmodernists, on the other hand, are right to empha-size freedom and uniqueness in history, but they treat history as if it were the outcome of arbitrary idealistic action, and, thus, they fail to recognize the kairic character of human action, which I delineated in Chapter 1.

As a conclusion, since history is created by the intentionality of consciousness, according to man's kairic action, the most adequate way of studying history consists in the study of the intentionality, and particularly of the kairicity, of the actors' conscious minds.

CHAPTER 3. COMMUNICATION AMONG CONSCIOUS BEINGS AND THE DYNAMICS OF THE ECONOMIC SYSTEM

As I have argued in Chapter 1, consciousness is not merely a framework within which the accumulation of experiences takes place, but it is an alive and structured presence that has all the characteristics of a being — namely: substance, structure, temporal and spatial activity — and it is continuously restructured, determining the laws of its activity, of its intentionality and of its integration into the world. Thus, consciousness is the fullest expression of the reality of the human being. Consciousness is both the ontological synopsis of the human being and the means by which the human being confirms its autonomy and its quest for other beings.

Conscious beings meet each other in the contexts of their conscious minds. This meeting takes place in accordance with the intentionality of consciousness and especially the kairicity of consciousness. The means by which conscious minds communicate with each other are called symbols. A symbol is a form that objectivates conscious beings' attempts to participate in each other's mental reality. Furthermore, symbols are forms that express commonly accepted intentions and actions and can be organized in sets that are called codes[63]. When conscious minds act and behave according to common codes, a society of conscious minds is an inter-subjective and conscious continuum.

As a code becomes more complete and more complex, it may increase the efficiency and the accuracy of the communication among conscious minds, but, on the other hand, it may make the communication among conscious minds more difficult. The elements of a code with which conscious minds communicate with each other are sings. Each and every sign receives a meaning that is related to its acceptance by each and every consciousness and to its participation in the overall code. Every code and every sign have a dynamic structure that makes it possible for them to be functionally adapted to various requests. The functional success of every system of communication depends on the extent to which and the manner in which it can comply with a generalized correspondence between the signifier and the signified[64].

---

63 The choice of a code depends on the following factors: (i) the convenience of codeword transmission (e.g. it is technically easier to use a binary code), (ii) the convenience of perception (e.g. machine codes are more convenient for processor operation), (iii) providing for maximum channel capacity (by the term communication channel, I mean a device with one input and one output), (iv) providing for noise-stability, and (v) providing for definite properties of an algorithm for encoding (e.g. encoding simplicity, unique decipherability, etc.).

64 According to Ferdinand de Saussure, language is made up of signs and every sign has two sides: (i) the signifier, i.e., the 'shape' of a word, its phonic component (the sequence of letters or phonemes, e.g. H-O-R-S-E), and (ii) the signified, the ideational component, the concept or object that appears in our minds when we hear or read the signifier. See: Hadumod Bussmann, *Routledge Dictionary of Language and Linguistics*, London: Routledge, 1996. However, the mathematician and philosopher René Thom, in his "Topologie et linguistique", argues that, if we restrict ourselves to a Saussurean view on language, then only one aspect of the sign seems amendable to objective description, namely the physical one, the signifier, whereas the signified is accessible only through introspection, and thus it escapes all third person determination. In Thom's view, this situation is paradoxical insofar as our folk understanding of language and the function that language serves call for a robust link between the signified (our meaning intentions, as Husserl would have put it) and the signifier. Hence, Thom's analysis is

At this point, we must clarify the difference between the terms 'meaning' and 'significance'. In addition to having a 'meaning', i.e., a denotation, or conceptual definition, every sign also has a 'significance', i.e., a mode of referring us to a being (or a collection of beings) that is denoted by the given sign, transcends the given sign and constitutes the correct interpretation of the given sign. The distinction between 'meaning' and 'significance' is originally due to the mathematician and philosopher Gottlob Frege, who suggested that, in addition to having a denotation, names and descriptions also express a 'sense', which is the way by which one conceives the denotation of the term. Frege's views about the distinction between 'meaning' and 'significance' were adopted by Wilhelm Dilthey, who applied them in the "mental" sciences, and by Ernst Troeltsch, who applied them in the social sciences. Moreover, Jaspers developed the distinction between 'explanation' and 'understanding' on the basis of the distinction between 'meaning' and 'significance'.

In its attempt to assign meanings and significances to things, consciousness has the continuous tendency to move toward two directions — an extrinsic one and an intrinsic one. When consciousness follows an intrinsic direction, the purposes of its action are to gain access to its own self in order to structure and experience it in a more complete manner and also to be sheltered in its own inner world and to strengthen its ontological status by itself. In this way, a being becomes deeper and, by refusing to widen itself, avoids the

---

focused on the encoding of pre-linguistic representations in language. This problem has two aspects: (i) representations, or the signifiers, are endowed with a structure that precedes their linguistic articulation; (ii) if such representations are to be expressed faithfully, then language must dispose of semantic forms by means of which it can express these structures. In the context of Thom's analysis, the Saussurean transformation from an amorphous signified to a formed signifier, which remains opaque within the framework of Saussure's theory, can be readdressed as follows: we can consider the level of the signified as a structured domain, a morphology of meaning, and therefore consider the signified-signifier relation as a mapping of this morphology onto the morphology of language. See: René Thom, *Mathematical Models of Morphogenesis*, trans. W.M. Brookes and D. Rand, Chichester: Ellis Horwood Ltd, 1983, ch. 11.

danger of wasting its potential. However, this entrenchment in the inner ego cannot secure the integration of a being, because every being is characterized not only by its autonomy but also by its participation in other beings. If consciousness persists in intensifying its inner ego, then the inner ego inhibits the manifestation of the social ego, and, therefore, the social ego is unable to strengthen the conscious person through a dialectical relationship with other conscious persons.

In its attempt to endow things with meanings and significances, the ego needs assistance from and cooperation with other egos. The existence of symbols and signs corresponds to the need of the ego to be complemented by other egos. Symbols and signs specify the relations among conscious beings that partake of common aesthetic experiences or exchange information with each other. Thus, consciousness runs two risks: the risk of over-information, which is associated with extremely high information entropy[65], and the risk of

---

65 In general, according to the *Oxford Dictionary of Science* (2005), 'entropy' is "a measure of the unavailability of a system's energy to do work; also a measure of disorder; the higher the entropy the greater the disorder". In information theory, the concept of 'entropy' was originally devised by Claude Shannon in 1948 to study the amount of information in a transmitted message: in this case, 'entropy' is the average amount of data deficit ('Shannon's uncertainty') that the informee (i.e., the person/ the machine for whom/ which a message is intended) has before the inspection of the output of the informer (i.e., the producer of the given message). In fact, in his famous article "A Mathematical Theory of Communication" (*Bell System Technical Journal*, Vol. 27, 1948, pp. 379-423, 623-656), Shannon laid down the basic elements of communication: an information source that produces a message; a transmitter that operates on the message to create a signal which can be sent through a channel; a channel, which is the medium over which the signal, carrying the information that composes the message, is sent; a receiver, which transforms the signal back into the message intended for delivery; and a destination, which can be a person or a machine for whom or which the message is intended. Following Shannon, W. Weaver, in his article "The Mathematics of Communication" (*Scientific American*, Vol. 181, 1949, pp. 11-15), presented a tripartite analysis of information in terms of: (1) technical problems concerning the quantification of information and dealt by Shannon's theory, (2) semantic problems relating to meaning and truth, and (3) what he called "influential" problems concerning the impact and effectiveness of information on human behav-

under-information, which is associated with extremely low information entropy. Over-information intensifies the social ego and, by increasing information entropy, leads to a disorientated being. Under-information intensifies the inner ego and leads to an ego-centric being. The risks of over-information and under-information can be avoided by following the four-fold dialectic of kairicity, which I defined in Chapter 1.

The economic system is a particular case of the general phenomenon of the communication among conscious beings. If we leave the realm of unconscious interdependence — which is the realm of classical and neoclassical microeconomics — and attempt to deal with problems of deliberate cooperation, we need a new way of theorizing about economic organizations based on kairicity. In the sequel, I shall study the states to which an economic organization is attracted — namely: (i) stable equilibrium, (ii) instability, and (iii) kairic point.

Stable equilibrium: If we follow the terminology used by Chester Barnard[66], then an economic organization is a "system of consciously coordinated activities or forces of two or more persons". The following conditions are necessary for organization to emerge: (i) persons must be willing to contribute actively to the (cooperative) system; (ii) they must share a common goal; (iii) deliberate communication must be possible and present. The first two conditions must be met if the pattern is to be considered consciously cooperative, and the third condition must be met if conscious coordination and hence organization is to emerge. Herbert Simon[67] has argued that the cooperative pattern emerges when the participants prefer the same set of consequences. If anticipations concerning one another's behavior are correct, then all will act (cooperate) to secure these consequences. Nevertheless, in the absence of deliberate communication, the pattern tends to be highly unstable. Thus, conscious

---

ior. For more details, see: Luciano Floridi, "Information", in L. Floridi (ed.), *The Blackwell Guide to the Philosophy of Computing and Information*, Oxford: Blackwell, 2003, pp. 40-61, and the references therein.

66 Chester Barnard, *The Functions of the Executive*, Cambridge, MA: Harvard University Press, 1938.

67 H.A. Simon, *Administrative Behavior*, New York: Macmillan, 1947.

coordination is the device or process whereby each participant is informed as to the strategies selected by the others. The process of communication within the formal system of an organization is specialized in fairly stable centers of communication that make up the executive body of the given organization. However, the executive is not a mere center of communication, but it also yields authority over the members of the organization, i.e., the executive function implies the issuing of coordinating and authoritative communications to those who contribute activities to the organization.

The formal system of an organization aims mainly at carrying out established, repetitive, day-to-day activities as efficiently as possible, and, therefore, it must function according to well-defined hierarchical structures and strictly applied rules and procedures. An efficient formal system in an organization is necessarily based on the non-ephemeral character of at least part of the interactions that are included in the organization, and, thus, it is meant to resist change and sustain the status quo to secure efficiency. Hence, the formal system of any successful organization is orderly and stable[68]. The formal system of an organization is pulled toward stable equilibrium by the forces of integration, maintenance controls and the need to adapt to the environment[69].

The informal system of an organization refers to a culture primarily satisfying the human desire for security, certainty and conformity (it is not only this, however, as I shall show later). In case the above-mentioned pull of the formal system of an organization

---

68 The concepts of stability and instability are studied in the theory of dynamical systems. A dynamical system is a mathematical formalization for any fixed rule that describes the time dependence of a point's position in a geometric space. A motion or its orbit is said to be 'stable' if the effect of small disturbances on the motion or its orbit is small. A motion or its orbit is said to be 'unstable' if the effect of small disturbances on the motion or its orbit is significant. A motion or its orbit is said to be 'asymptotically stable' if the effect of small disturbances on the motion or its orbit tends to disappear. For a mathematically rigorous study of these concepts, see: Nicolas Laos, *Topics in Mathematical Analysis and Differential Geometry*, London: World Scientific Publishing Co., 1998.

69 See: P.R. Lawrence and J.W. Lorsch, *Organization and Environment*, Cambridge, MA: Harvard University Press, 1967.

toward stable equilibrium is reinforced by the informal system, then the given organization as a whole will be attracted to stability. Negative feedback[70] drives both formal and informal systems; in this case, 'negative feedback' refers to the law of diminishing marginal utility[71] or to the law of diminishing returns.

As a conclusion, in the absence of strong destabilizing conscious and/ or unconscious causes, organizations seem to be attracted to a stable bureaucratic state in which they carry on doing the same thing: this is the point emphasized by classical and neoclassical microeconomics[72].

Instability: Whereas all organizations are pulled to stability, they are simultaneously pulled to instability by powerful forces of division and decentralization[73]. If the formal systems of an organization move too far in the direction of division and decentralization, then they become fragmented and unstable[74]. Moreover, even if the formal systems of an organization do not move so far in this direction, the informal systems of an organization are pulled toward instability by even more powerful forces. It should be mentioned that informal systems are a device not only for security and conformity but also for satisfying human desires for innovation, individuality (experience of existential 'otherness') and isolation from the environment. If informal systems are dominated by behavior patterns that refer to innovation, individuality and isolation from the environment, then they pull the entire organization to fragmentation

---

70 By the term 'feedback', we mean a situation when output from an event in the past will influence an occurrence or occurrences of the same event in the present or future.

71 According to the law of diminishing marginal utility, "as the amount of a good consumed increases, the marginal utility of that good tends to diminish". See: Samuelson and Nordhaus, *Economics*, p. 84.

72 For more details, see: Danny Miller, *The Icarus Paradox: How Excellent Organizations Can Bring About Their Own Downfall*, New York: Harper Business, 1990; R.T. Pascale, *Managing at the Edge: How Successful Companies Use Conflict to Stay Ahead*, London: Viking Press, 1990; Samuelson and Nordhaus, *Economics*.

73 See: Lawrence and Lorsch, *Organization and Environment*.

74 See: Miller, *The Icarus Paradox*.

and instability. Thus, in organizational terms, the attractor to instability means that positive feedback[75] behavior, such as political interaction and organizational defense mechanisms, cause disorder in the system[76].

Kairic point: The alternative to either stability or instability lies in the border between them — namely, at a kairic point — where both negative and positive feedback, both stability and instability, operate simultaneously to cause the emergence of changing patterns of behavior. In organizational terms, at a kairic point, the formal systems operate in a stable way to secure efficient operations on a daily basis whereas the informal system operates in a destabilizing manner to cause change. For an organization to be changeable and hence innovative, its informal system — namely, the shifting network of social and other informal contacts between people within an organization and across its borders — must operate according to the dialectic of kairicity[77].

An informal network operates according to the dialectic of kairicity when opposing ways of behaving are simultaneously present. For instance, there is 'instability' when an organization experiences the clash of countercultures, the tensions of political activity, or when some managers operate in the formal organization using capital-budgeting techniques to keep the organization stable while, at the same time, others operate in the informal system to get around those budgetary controls, etc.[78] If an organization is attracted only

75 A system is said to exhibit 'positive feedback', in response to perturbation, if it acts to increase the magnitude of the perturbation. In social-economic systems, positive feedback effects may also be referred to as 'virtuous' or 'vicious' cycles.

76 See: Chris Argyris, *Overcoming Organizational Defenses: Facilitating Organizational Learning*, Boston: Allen & Bacon, Prentice-Hall, 1990.

77 See: R.D. Stacey, *Strategic Management and Organizational Dynamics*, London: Pitman, 1993.

78 See: Ikujiro Nonaka, "Creating Organizational Order Out of Chaos: Self-renewal in Japanese Firms", *California Management Review*, Vol. 30, 1988, pp. 57-73; M.M. Waldrop, *Complexity: The Emerging Science at the Edge of Order and Chaos*, London: Viking, 1992.

to the state of behavior that we call stability, then it will stop being creative; in fact, Cornelius Castoriadis has argued that:

> [I]f the system were actually able to change individuals into things moved only by economic 'forces', it would collapse not in the long run, but immediately. The struggle of people against re-ification is, just as much as the tendency toward reification, the condition for the functioning of capitalism. A factory in which the workers were really and totally mere cogs in the machine, blindly executing the orders of management, would come to a stop in a quarter of an hour.[79]

If an organization is attracted only to the state of behavior that we call instability, then it will be dissolved. An organization can remain simultaneously orderly and changeable if and only if the dis-orderly dynamics of conflict and dialogue — which are the founda-tions of changeability and hence of innovation — produce a viable new synthesis (conscious communication), i.e., if and only if it op-erates according to the dialectic of kairicity.

When one studies patterns of consumer behavior[80], 'negative feedback' is analogous to diminishing marginal utility; 'positive feedback' to increasing marginal utility. The Hollywood, the mass media and the advertising industry tend to make consumers behave under conditions of increasing marginal utility. Thus, demand can get out of control, since it is deliberately and continuously stimu-lated by the cultural context. We gain added insight into the sig-nificance of positive feedback for the explanation of patterns of consumer behavior by analyzing specific aspects of the so-called su-per-industrial economy[81]. First of all, in the super-industrial era, the production and control of what D. Bell calls "codified knowledge" — namely, systematic, coordinated information — is the main stra-tegic resource on which the economy depends. Those who are con-

---

79 Cornelius Castoriadis, *The Imaginary Institution of Society*, London: Polity Press, 1987 (originally published in 1975 by Éditions du Seuil), p. 16.

80 See: Brian Mullen and Craig Johnson, *The Psychology of Consumer Behavior*, New Jersey: Lawrence Erlbaum, 1990.

81 See: Daniel Bell, *The Coming of Post-Industrial Society*, New York: Basic Books, 1973; Alvin Toffler, *The Third Wave*, London: Pan, 1981; Alain Touraine, *The Post-Industrial Society*, London: Wilwood, 1974; Raymond Williams, *Towards 2000*, Harmondsworth: Penguin, 1985.

cerned with the creation and distribution of "codified knowledge" — namely, scientists, managers/ economists and skilled professionals of all kinds — increasingly become the leading social groups, often replacing the entrepreneurs of the old system[82]. Hence, in the super-industrial economy, the consumers who spend on education and professional-training programs in order to acquire more knowledge and more professional skills operate under the conditions of increasing marginal utility. In fact, in the super-industrial era, the need for life-long, continuous education/ training shows the significance of positive-feedback analysis for the explanation of consumer behavior.

Furthermore, the significance of positive-feedback analysis for the explanation of consumer behavior is increased by the fact that the products of the so-called 'new economy', such as operational systems for PCs, mobile-phone sets, music CDs, iPods, etc., as well as many products of the so-called 'old economy', such as cars, are characterized by a high level of inherent obsolescence — namely, these products become obsolete very quickly and those who buy them are continuously pushed to buy new/ updated products.

In classical and neoclassical partial-equilibrium analysis[83], the idea of a single equilibrium is encouraged by the law of diminishing returns. This one-sided single-equilibrium explanation of the law is wrong, especially in the context of the 'new economy' industries. Computers, software, optical fibers and telecommunications equipment, medical electronics and pharmaceuticals are all subject to increasing returns. This is because, from the outset, they necessitate enormous outlays on Research and Development, designing and redesigning, developing a prototype and setting up tools and automated plants for manufacture. But, once the products start rolling off the production line, the cost of producing additional units of

---

82 See: J.K. Galbraith, *American Capitalism*, Boston: Houghton Mifflin, 1952.
83 'Partial-equilibrium analysis' means "analysis concentrating on the effect of changes in an individual market, holding other things equal, (e.g. disregarding changes in income)", whereas 'general-equilibrium analysis' refers to "an equilibrium state for the economy as a whole in which the markets for all goods and services are simultaneously in equilibrium"; see: Samuelson and Nordhaus, *Economics*, pp. 737, 743.

output drops very sharply in relation to the initial investment[84] (e.g. software — once written, tested, debugged and enhanced — is very cheap to duplicate, and it can become a massive source of continuous ever-increasing returns, until the producers bring out a better version).

The many input and output markets are connected in an interdependent system that can be conceived in terms of a Boolean network[85]. A Boolean network consists of a number of elements, or cells. Each cell is connected to others and sends outputs to all or some of those others. What state each cell is in at any moment — namely, what it is outputting at any moment — depends on the inputs it is receiving and the rules it follows to respond to those inputs. Thus, the state of an individual cell changes from moment to moment according to the energy or information it receives and the rules it follows for converting inputs into output.

Suppose that each cell in the network is randomly connected to others and randomly assigned a different decision-making rule. Moreover, suppose that we assign randomly different initial conditions. When every cell is connected to every other, then the whole system is attracted to instability: it behaves randomly, and any time change in the initial pattern from which the system is started will lead to completely different subsequent patterns over time. However, when each cell is connected to only two others and random decision rules are assigned to all the cells, the whole system is attracted to stability: random local rules of behavior can cause the emergence of order at a global level, and whether there is order or not depends on the degree of connectedness between cells of the network. Furthermore, it should be mentioned that, just before such systems go completely random, i.e., at a kairic point, they behave in a different

---

84 See: Georges Anderla, Anthony Dunning and Simon Forge, *Chaotics*, Twickenham: Adamantine Press, 1997.

85 See: S.A. Kauffman, "Antichaos and Adaptation", *Scientific American*, August 1991, pp. 78-84; S.A. Kauffman, *Origins of Order: Self-organization and Selection in Evolution*, Oxford: Oxford University Press, 1993.

manner: coherent structures that grow, split apart, and recombine in different patterns[86] due to the dialectic of kairicity.

---

86 For a mathematically rigorous study of these patterns, see: Stephen Wolfram, "Computer Software in Science and Mathematics", *Scientific American*, September 1986, pp. 188-203.

CHAPTER 4. ECONOMIC ASSUMPTIONS

According the positivist-empiricist tradition[87], a theory is a set of generalizations about the behavior of the world, and the real test of a scientific theory is its ability to predict. In other words, for positivism-empiricism, prediction is the true criterion of whether a particular theory is correct or not. Working within the positivist-empiricist tradition, Milton Friedman, the founder of a neoclassical school of economic thought known as the "Chicago school of economics", formulated an instrumentalist explanation of economic assumptions[88]. For Friedman, the theory is an instrument of prediction, and, therefore, the value of a theory is determined by its ability to predict observable phenomena.

---

87 See: C.G. Hempel, *Aspects of Concept Formation in Empirical Science*, Chicago: University of Chicago Press, 1965; Imre Lakatos, "Falsification and the Methodology of Scientific Research Programmes", in I. Lakatos and A. Musgrave (eds), *Criticism and the Growth of Knowledge*, Cambridge: Cambridge University Press, 1970; K.R. Popper, *The Logic of Scientific Discovery*, New York: Harper & Collins, 1959.
88 Milton Friedman, *Essays in Positive Economics*, Chicago: University of Chicago Press, 1953.

Jarrett Leplin[89] extended Friedman's instrumentalism by arguing for scientific realism, i.e., the view that the world described by science is the real world. For Leplin, the best explanation of a theory's having reliable prediction about a range of phenomena is that its assumptions are objectively true. In contrast to Friedman's and Leplin's epistemological arguments that, in Chapter 1, I argued that the world conception of science is not a 'world' more than it is a 'conception'. Furthermore, in the light of the arguments I have put forward up to this point, the fact that all nonlinear feedback systems — such as firms, economic sectors, etc. — can be studied in terms of deterministic systems does not imply that economic behavior should be explained in similar ways to natural (i.e., inanimate) behavior.

For instance, every human organization is a deterministic nonlinear feedback system[90] because it is characterized by decision-making rules and by specific interpersonal relations among the people who belong to the same organization or to different organi-

---

89 Jarrett Leplin, *Scientific Realism*, Berkeley: University of California Press, 1984.
90 The feedback loops that are created by people when they interact with each other, i.e., when they form a network, are nonlinear because of the following reasons: (i) in human systems, the actors' choices are based on subjective perceptions which lead to disproportionately big or small reactions; (ii) there are almost always many possible outcomes that can follow an action; (iii) due to the action of structural forces, group behavior is something more than the mere sum of individual behaviors; (iv) outcomes are usually individual; (v) small changes can escalate and lead to outcomes of major significance. Hence, the assumption of nonlinearity is necessary in order to formulate models that can account for the previous five characteristics of human systems. On the other hand, the prevailing models of classical and neoclassical economics are based on linear models. Thus, Daniel Hausman attempted to defend scientific realism in the field of economic theory by arguing that the goal for the economist is to arrive at assumptions that are approximately true (Daniel Hausman, *The Inexact and Separate Science of Economics*, Cambridge: Cambridge University Press, 1992). However, Hausman remains anchored in the conviction of classical and neoclassical economic thought to a deterministic model that underestimates the economic actors' freedom of choice and fails to recognize the dynamic continuity between consciousness and the world.

zations — in fact, this is what we mean by the term 'institutional framework'. In any deterministic nonlinear feedback system, actors must necessarily move around nonlinear feedback loops, which are formed by the corresponding institutional framework, and it is exactly for this reason that the system within which actors act is deterministic. On the other hand, every time an actor moves around such a loop, he is free to transform, ignore or even overthrow the given institutional framework, because actors follow decision-making rules and specific models of behavior, but these rules and these models allow freedom of choice, i.e., they are subject to change (this is why, for instance, human history includes business innovations, social revolutions, changes in legislation, changes in morals and customs, etc.). Therefore, on the one hand, economic actors cannot escape from the fact that the interactions among them have the character of a nonlinear feedback system and also they cannot escape from the consequences of this nonlinear feedback, but, on the other hand, economic actors can, indeed, change the rules and the patterns that govern their behavior on different occasions, in accordance with their intentionality. The consequences that free choice has for the system can be divided into the following three categories:

(i) Stable outcomes: If all economic actors accept a given set of decision rules and make their choices according to these rules, then the whole system will end up in a state of stable equilibrium (i.e., it will exhibit a 'regular' behavior). In this case, the economic system operates on the basis of negative feedback, which underpins the exhibition of regular, predictable behavior.

(ii) Unstable outcomes: When all economic actors continuously change the rules that govern their behavior, then none of them will be able to depend on others, and the whole system will be attracted to a state of unstable equilibrium due to positive feedback. In other words, as the level of conflict ('social entropy') increases in a human system, then this system leaves a state in which it is attracted to stability and moves toward a state in which it is attracted to a behavior of unstable equilibrium. In particular, when 'paradox'[91] becomes the central issue of economic analysis, economic actors are treated as systems out of equilibrium, and their dynamics are characterized by disorder and evolve through political processes[92] according to a dialectic manner[93] and exhibit a series of crises[94].

(iii) Kairic state: When a nonlinear feedback system operates in a state characterized by kairicity, then its behavior is simultaneously characterized by stability and instability: it is unstable, in the sense that it does not obey quantitative generalizations, and hence long-term predictions are impossible, and it is stable, in the sense that there is an identifiable qualitative structure in this behavior.

91 See: Charles Hampden-Turner, *Charting the Corporate Mind*, New York: Free Press/ Macmillan, 1990.
92 See: Andrew Pettigrew, *The Awaking Giant*, Oxford: Blackwell, 1985.
93 See: Pascale, *Managing at the Edge*.
94 See: Miller, *The Icarus Paradox*.

CHAPTER 5. INSUFFICIENT ECONOMIC ASSUMPTIONS AND THE PROBLEM OF UNEMPLOYMENT

'Classical unemployment'

According to this assumption, unemployment results from too high real wages. In other words, workers are unemployed because real wages are too high. Therefore, according to this assumption, if workers work harder and go on strike less often, then productivity will be increased, and increased productivity will increase the international competitiveness of the given country's economy, and, therefore, finally, more jobs will be created and the Gross Domestic Product per capita will rise.

The previous analysis is partially true. A more careful inquiry into the notion of productivity indicates that productivity has very little to do with recipes for harder work or lower real wages. Harder work and cuts in real wages cannot by themselves cause a significant increase in productivity. Significant increases in productivity can be achieved through organizational improvement and technological progress. Thus, low productivity is primarily due to poor management and narrow-minded approaches to economics.

Laissez-faire capitalism

Early classical economists were of course aware of business cycles, but they viewed these as temporary and self-correcting. Their analysis was based on the reasoning that underpins 'Say's law of markets'. In 1803, the French economist and businessman Jean-Baptiste Say formulated the so-called Say's law of markets, according to which overproduction is impossible by its very nature. In James Mill's *Commerce Defended* (1808), Say's law of market is expressly set forth as follows: "The production of commodities creates, and is the one and universal cause that creates a market for the commodities produced"[95]. According to John Maynard Keynes, the essence of Say's law of markets is that "supply creates its own demand in the sense that the aggregate demand price is equal to the aggregate supply price for all levels of output and employment"[96].

Many distinguished economists, such as D. Ricardo, J.S. Mill, A. Marshall and A.C. Pigou, subscribed to the classical macroeconomic view that overproduction is impossible. In particular, Pigou has put forward the following argument:

> With perfectly free competition there will always be a strong tendency toward full employment. Such unemployment as exists at any time is due wholly to the fictional resistances [that] prevent the appropriate wage and price adjustments being made instantaneously.[97]

P.A. Samuelson and W.D. Nordhaus have explained the rationale behind this classical view as follows:

> wages and prices are sufficiently flexible that markets will 'clear', or return to equilibrium, very quickly. If prices and wages adjust rapidly, then the short-run in which prices are sticky will be so short that it can be neglected for all practical purposes. The classical macroeconomics conclude that the economy always operates at full employment or at its potential output... Macroeconomic aggregate demand policies cannot influence the level of unemployment and output. Rather, monetary and

---

95 James Mill, *Commerce Defended*, Gloucester: Dodo Press, 2008 (originally published in 1808), chapter VI: Consumption.
96 J.M. Keynes, *The General Theory of Employment, Interest and Money*, London: Macmillan, 2007 (originally published in 1936), chapter 2, section VII
97 A.C. Pigou, *The Theory of Unemployment*, New York: A.M. Kelley, 1968 (originally published in 1933).

> fiscal policies can affect only the economy's price level, along
> with the composition of the real GNP...At the heart of the clas-
> sical view is the belief that prices and wages are flexible and
> that price flexibility provides a self-correcting mechanism that
> quickly restores full employment and always maintains poten-
> tial output.[98]

On the other hand, historical experience has proved that the previous classical view is wrong. For instance, during the Great Depression, when a quarter of the American labor force was unemployed, classical macroeconomics were unable to explain the situation: a vast number of workers was unemployed for a long period of time even though wages and prices were flexible, and, in fact, unemployed workers were begging for work and selling pencils on street corners. Indeed, a laissez-faire policy may need more time to correct the problem of unemployment and can be successful in the long run, by leading to the emergence of new industries and jobs, but, if it allows unemployment to rise at high levels, then, in social, psychological and political terms, it is extremely risky[99].

Keynesian economics

In contrast to the assumptions of classical economics, Keynes's *General Theory* argued that prices and wages are inflexible or sticky and, therefore, at least in the short-run, the economy may not automatically cure itself of recessionary gap, i.e., it may not be self-regulating. In particular, Keynes argued that employees will naturally resist employers' efforts to cut wages and, in general, labor unions may resist wage cuts; hence, wages may be inflexible in a downward direction. In addition, Keynes argued that, as a result of the existence of anti-competitive or monopolistic forces, the internal

---

98 Samuelson and Nordhaus, *Economics*, pp. 465, 466.
99 See: A.W. Clark, "The Effects of Unemployment on Political Attitude", *Journal of Sociology*, Vol. 21, 1985, pp. 100–108; N.T. Feather, *The psychological Impact of Unemployment*, New York: Springer-Verlag, 1990; David Fryer and Philip Ullah (eds), *Unemployed People: Social and Psychological Perspectives*, Milton Keynes: Open University Press, 1987; Catherine Hakim, "The Social Consequences of High Unemployment", *Journal of Social Policy*, Vol. 11, 1982, pp. 433-467; Marie Jahoda, *Employment and Unemployment: A Social-Psychological Analysis*, Cambridge: Cambridge University Press, 1982.

structure of an economy is not necessarily competitive enough to allow prices to adjust according to the assumptions of the classical economists. Thus, "Keynes emphasized that because wages and prices are inflexible", "there is no self-correcting mechanism", and, therefore, "a nation could remain in its low-output, high-misery condition for a long time"[100].

At this point, it must be mentioned that so-called 'New Keynesian economists' have argued that the inflexibility of wages is primarily due to solid microeconomic reasons, in the sense that labor productivity depends on the wage rate that the firm pays its employees, and, therefore, a cut in wages can cause labor productivity to decline, which, in turn, raises the firm's costs.

Furthermore, in contrast to Say's law, Keynes argued that added saving will not necessarily stimulate an equal amount of added investment spending[101]. In particular, Keynes argued that individuals save and invest for a host of reasons, and, therefore, no single factor, such as interest rate, determines the relation between these activities. Hence, for Keynes, if, at a given price level, total spending falls, so will aggregate demand; i.e., saving could increase and aggregate demand could fall. Additionally, Keynes argued that saving is more responsive to changes in income than to changes in the interest rate and that investment is more responsive to technological changes, business expectations and innovations than to changes in the interest rate.

As a result of his previous observations, Keynes proposed a new model of economic policy, which can be summarized as follows:

> through monetary or fiscal policies, the government can stimulate the economy and help maintain high levels of output and employment...These policies might increase aggregate demand

---

100 Samuelson and Nordhaus, *Economics*, p. 466.

101 According to Say's law, if consumption spending falls because saving increases, then total spending will not fall because the added saving will cause an increase in investment spending through changes in the interest rate. In particular, according to classical macroeconomic analysis, the added saving will cause a reduction in the interest rate, and, at a lower interest rate, businesses will borrow and invest more. Hence, from this viewpoint, through changes in the interest rate, the amount of saving will always be equal to the amount invested.

in periods of slow economic activity or curb spending in periods of boom with threatening inflation. The Keynesian economist might argue that government spending crowds out[102] nothing at all because higher government spending increases output and allows private spending to continue. In essence, when the government takes a larger slice out of the pie, the pie actually becomes larger. Government spending, tax cuts, or more rapid money growth — all create more output and thus stimulate investment.[103]

However, Keynes's theory has the following three major weaknesses:

(i) In his general theory, Keynes has specified the direction in which his monetary and fiscal policies are likely to work, but he has not made predictions about their precise outcome and the time-lags involved. In fact, the precise outcomes of Keynesian monetary and fiscal policies and the time-lags involved are uncertain because private investment is greatly dependent on uncertain psychological and cultural factors (i.e., on the moods and cultural characteristics of the investors) and because the balance of trade (exports minus imports) is largely dependent on external factors.

(ii) Not all unemployment is 'cyclical'[104], i.e., not all unemployment is caused by demand deficiency. Unemployment may be 'structural' — namely, unemployment may be caused not by lack of demand, but by changes in demand patterns or obsolescence of technology. If most of the unemployment is structural, then the correction of the problem of unemployment requires retraining of workers and large investment in new capital equipment. Moreover, if most of the unemployment is structural, then most of the increase

---

102 "Classical economists would worry about government spending crowd-ing out private production. By 'crowding out', they mean that when the government increases its spending, production on private goods will be displaced"; see: Samuelson and Nordhaus, *Economics*, p. 467.

103 Samuelson and Nordhaus, *Economics*, pp. 466, 477.

104 Cyclical or Keynesian unemployment is a situation in which there are unemployed workers not because there is inadequate capital equip-ment for them to combine with, but because there is not enough ag-gregate demand in the economy to absorb the output which could be produced.

in spending is absorbed into price increases (thus causing 'demand-pull inflation') rather than generating greater real output[105].

(iii) Keynesianism is focused on the problem of unemployment — which was the great economic plague of his era — but, after the 1950s, governments have become increasingly concerned not only with the stabilization of a high employment level but also with the stabilization of prices and the balance of payments. Moreover, the increasing internationalization of trade undermines the effectiveness of Keynesianism: expansion of demand in order to lower unemployment may lead to a faster expansion of imports than exports, and, therefore, it may lead to a deterioration of the balance of payments, to which governments may respond by reducing taxation (and public spending) or by raising interest rates.

Monetarism

According to monetarism, which was founded by Milton Friedman, unemployment is mainly due to the following factors: (i) low competitiveness of the economy, (ii) overvalued products, and (iii) the undermining of entrepreneurship by inflation, high taxation and excessive government spending. Hence, monetarists try to correct the problem of unemployment by eliminating non-productive economic organizations, reducing inflation and taxation (in conjunction with reducing government spending), and creating a business environment that encourages entrepreneurship, thus leading to the creation of new business activities, which will increase employment.

How do monetarists believe that the previous sequence of events will be achieved? The answer that they give is that the volume of money must be reduced and thus its value must rise. Let us

---

105 In September 1976, in the U.K., a Labor Prime Minister, Jim Callaghan, told his party conference: "We used to think you could spend your way out of a recession and increase employment by cutting taxes and boosting government spending. I tell you in all candour that the option no longer exists and that in so far as it did ever exist, it only worked by injecting inflation into the economy. And each time that happened, the average level of unemployment has risen. Higher inflation followed by higher unemployment. That is the history of the last twenty years".

give an example. Assume that the Fed allows the interest rate to rise and generally follows a tough and credible monetary policy, so that the value of U.S. dollar rises. This event will increase the purchasing power of the U.S. dollar abroad, and, therefore, imports will become cheaper to Americans and they will buy more from foreigners. This event, in turn, will cause a reduction in inflation. Simultaneously, the increase in interest rates will reduce both borrowing and consumption. Furthermore, as the value of the dollar rises[106], American export prices increase. Hence, inefficient producers in the U.S. will encounter a double threat: reduced foreign demand for their products and increased competition in the domestic market, since imports become cheaper. Unless inefficient U.S. companies manage to improve their efficiency, they will have to shut down their production. Monetarists argue that, in order to reduce inflation, the government must reduce its spending and increase the interest rate. A decrease in government spending increases competition in the domestic economy, and an increase in interest rates makes it even more difficult for companies that have liquidity problems to survive under increasing competition.

In principle, the previous monetarist approach is logically sound. On the other hand, in practice, it is only partially true, because some of its assumptions are wrong. The biggest defect of monetarism is its inability to distinguish between the total economic system and the circulation of money as a subsystem of the total economic system. This conceptual weakness of monetarism leads to two major problems:

(i) First, the effectiveness of monetarist policies is lower than their advocates have hoped, because the monetary system is not a closed national system. The first internationally acclaimed book on

---

106 A currency offering a high interest rate often attracts buying of that currency, and therefore the exchange rate on that currency rises. For instance, a significant rise in the dollar "began in 1980 after a tight monetary policy and loose fiscal policy in the U.S., drove interest rates up sharply. High interest rates, a conservative administration in the United States, and a cut in the U.S. tax rates attracted mobile funds from other currencies to U.S. dollars"; see: Samuelson and Nordhaus, *Economics*, p. 717.

international political economy, Spero's *Politics of International Economic Relations*[107], focused on OECD interdependence, East-West interdependence and southern dependence on the north. Samuelson and Nordhaus have made the following observations:

> In a world where economies are increasingly linked by trade and capital flows, interdependence is unavoidable. No walls can prevent domestic actions from spilling over territorial boundaries. National strengths can be leveraged in global marketplace, while national weaknesses fall prey to intense foreign competitors...All this means that exchange with other nations is an integral part of domestic economic welfare.[108]

Furthermore, the rapid globalization of the international economy (especially in the areas of production and finance) and the changing nature of the interstate system in the post-Cold War era contribute to the emergence of a 'global' (as opposed to 'international') political economy. According to R. Cox, global political economy refers to "an economic space transcending all country borders, which co-exists still with an international economy based on transactions across country borders and which is regulated by inter-state agreements and practices"[109]. Thus, global political economy identifies three different levels of economic space — namely, supra-regional, national and sub-regional — and at least three different levels of social organization — namely, social forces, states (national societies) and global society[110].

(ii) An increase in the cost of capital may have very negative consequences for new companies in the initial phase of their operation, and, therefore, it may undermine productivity and inhibit the creation of new jobs. In the short-run, an increase in the cost of capital reduces inflation. But, if it is allowed to destroy new companies and to undermine future productivity, then it may generate phenomena of inefficiency and inflationary pressures. This means

---

107 Joan Spero, *The Politics of International Economic Relations*, London: Allen and Unwin, and New York: St Martin's Press, 1990.

108 Samuelson and Nordhaus, *Economics*, pp. 721-722.

109 Robert Cox, "Structural Issues of Global Governance: Implications for Europe", in S. Gill (ed.), *Gramsci, Historical Materialism and International Relations*, Cambridge: Cambridge University Press, 1993, pp. 259-289.

110 Ibid.

that the application of strict monetarist policies may cause serious recession either because these policies are extremely rigid or because the application of such policies lacks discretion. In other words, a major mistake of many monetarist economic stabilization programs is that they are characterized by a narrow focus on spending cuts, as if all spending is equal. This is wrong. Some spending goes to legitimate purposes and some goes to activities that are inefficient and undermine employment. Economic stabilization programs should be characterized by discretion, cutting the spending that goes directly to inefficient and job-killing activities. Monetarism is catastrophic and self-defeating if it is viewed as a dogma and not as a tool used by the kairicity of consciousness.

Protectionism

An alternative approach to the problem of unemployment is based on protectionism. First of all, temporary tariff protection for an 'infant industry' with growth potential may be an efficient policy. In his famous Report on Manufacturers (1791), Alexander Hamilton had argued that the growth of manufacturing should be encouraged by protecting youthful industries from foreign competition. The rationale of this protectionist policy, which has been cautiously supported by several free-market economists, like John Stuart Mill and Alfred Marshall, is that there are lines of production in which a country could have comparative advantage if only they were given the adequate opportunity to get started. History indicates that there are cases of infant industries that, after a period of tariff protection, grew up to stand on their own feet and that newly industrialized countries, such as Singapore and South Korea, have often protected their manufacturing industries from imports during the initial phase of industrialization. On the other hand, history indicates that there are also contrary cases in which infant industries were protected for long periods of time but they did not grow up to stand on their own feet[111]. Hence, the policy of protect-

---

111 See for instance: Samuelson and Nordhaus, *Economics*.

ing infant industries from imports must be applied according to the dialectic of kairicity.

Furthermore, protectionism often takes the form of retaliatory tariffs. The essence of this argument is "mutual trade": even though a country may agree that free trade is the best of all possible trade systems, it is justified to retaliate when a foreign country raises tariffs. This rationale was endorsed by the U.S. government in 1982 (in the Economic Report of the President):

> Intervention in international trade...even though costly to the U.S. economy in the short-run, may, however, be justified if it serves the strategic purpose of increasing the cost of interventionist policies by foreign governments. Thus, there is a potential role for carefully targeted measures...aimed at convincing other countries to reduce their trade distortions.

This argument should be used only within the framework of the dialectic of kairicity. If it is not used according to the dialectic of kairicity, then retaliatory tariffs can trigger trade wars. On the other hand, if the policy of retaliatory tariffs is applied according to the dialectic of kairicity, it can prevent the emergence of a mercantilist world of unilateral decisions and bilateral agreements.

Chapter 6. Insufficient Economic Assumptions and The Problem Of Inflation

Arthur M. Okun has argued that "the task of combining prosperity with price stability now stands as the major unsolved problem of aggregate economic performance"[112]. Both monetarism and 'orthodox' Keynesianism are based on Irving Fisher's 'equation[113] of exchange':

$$MV = PQ$$

where M is the quantity of money, V is the velocity of the circulation of money (i.e., the amount of nominal Gross National Product each year divided by the money stock), P is the price level, and Q is aggregate output (i.e., Gross National Product = PQ). Thus, according to Fisher, if both V and Q are constant, then a change in the money supply, M, results in an equal percentage change in the price level P.

The previous equation implies that

$$M = (1/V)PQ.$$

112 A.M. Okun, *The Political Economy of Prosperity*, New York: Norton, 1970, p. 130.
113 In fact, it is an identity.

Since V is constant, 1/V can be replaced by a constant k. Additionally, when the money market is in equilibrium, the demand for money, M_d is equal to M. Hence,

$M_d = kPQ$,

which means that, according to Fisher's model, the demand for money is a function of income and does not depend on interest rates.

However, in practice, the velocity of the circulation of money, V, is not constant, even in the short-run, and especially during periods of recession. In fact, Keynes extended Fisher's equation of exchange by pointing out there are three motives of holding money: (i) Transactions motive: money is a medium of exchange, and, as income rises, people have more transactions and hold more money. (ii) Precautionary motive: people hold money for emergencies, and money demand is again expected to rise with income. (iii) Speculative motive: money is also a way for people to store wealth, and, under the speculative motive, the demand for money is negatively related to the interest rate. Moreover, Keynes modeled the demand for money as the demand for the real (as opposed to the nominal) quantity of money (real balances), M/P. According to Keynes, the demand for real money balances is a function of both income and interest rates:

$M/P = f(Q, i)$,

where Q is output or income and i is the interest rate (and hence the velocity of the circulation of money fluctuates with the interest rate).

Milton Friedman[114], the founder of monetarism, restated Fisher's equation of exchange by arguing that, in the long run, output is determined only by real (non-monetary) factors and the velocity of the circulation of money is stable. Hence, from the standpoint of monetarism, Fisher's equation of exchange implies that control of the money supply provides a tool against inflation.

Fisher's equation of exchange, which plays a major role in both Keynesianism and monetarism, has an important defect — namely, it is based on the assumption that the monetary system is a closed national system. This assumption is wrong. Monetary policy influ-

---

114 Milton Friedman (ed.), *Studies in the Quantity Theory of Money*, Chicago: University of Chicago Press, 1956.

ences short-run national output if prices are sticky or if portfolio choices are not instantaneous, but it also affects output in other countries. For instance, in the Mundell-Fleming model, a monetary expansion in a foreign country reduces that country's real interest rate, depreciates its currency relative to others, raises import prices and raises inflation and output. But other countries are affected by this policy, too, because their currencies appreciate relative to the foreign country's (if, of course, they do not match the foreign country's monetary policy), thereby reducing import prices and inflation and possibly decreasing output[115].

In general, international capital mobility limits the effectiveness of monetary policy. For instance, any increase in aggregate demand caused by a reduction in domestic interest rates is partially dissipated in increased expenditures on imported goods financed by international capital flows. Furthermore, as it has been shown by Frenkel and Mussa[116], exchange rate adjustments that occur rapidly in response to perceived changes in monetary policy tend to lead to rapid adjustments of domestic prices and wages, thereby limiting the effect of monetary policy on output and employment.

Therefore, there is only one effective long-term cure for inflation: following the dialectic of kairicity, the economist must find the limiting factor or the limiting factors and devise ways to counter the negative consequences of inflation by increasing productivity or by finding substitute goods/ services.

115 Robert Mundell, "Notes on the History of the Mundell-Fleming Model: Keynote Speech", *Staff Papers, International Monetary Fund*, Vol. 47 (Special Issue), 2001, pp. 215-227.

116 J.A. Frenkel and M.L. Mussa, "Monetary and Fiscal Policies in an Open Economy", *American Economic Review*, Vol. 71, 1981, pp. 253-258.

Chapter 7. The Difficulties Of Refutation: The Development Of Knowledge In Economics

Classical economic thought is founded on an obsolete picture of natural sciences that was based on Cartesianism and Newtonian mechanics, and additionally it attempts to apply an obsolete notion of a 'scientific theory' to human systems without making any distinction between human systems and natural systems. As I have already argued in this book, not only is the epistemology of the classical economists obsolete but also their picture of natural science has been discarded by 20th century natural scientists. However, the following questions emerge[117]: Does economic theory contain substantive assumptions about the causal workings of the economic world that affect future observable states of the economic world? Furthermore, can we perform observations of states of the economic world that confirm or falsify the theory?

In principle, we are able to perform observations of states of the economic world that confirm or falsify the theory, once we agree on the definition of certain concepts. In fact, there are many cases —

---

117 See: D.W. Hands, *Testing, Rationality, and Progress: Essays on the Popperian Tradition in Economic Methodology*, Lanham, MD: Rowman & Littlefield Publishers, 1992.

e.g. theories of economic growth, unemployment, inflation, trade, etc. — in which we can describe the observations that would need to be secured to test these theories. The goal of 'positive economics' is to produce generalizations of the following type: if we observe the values of n variables V_i, where $i = 1,...,n$, i.e., of the n-tuple $V = (V_1, V_2,..., V_n)$, according to some observation rule R, then the observable n-tuple will satisfy the relations F_i, where $i = 1,...,m$. For convenience, I shall call every proposition of the previous deductive system a 'proposition of type A'.

Proposition of type A: For every observation, h, on the n-tuple V, if the observations h on V take place according to the observation rule R (i.e., the couples (h, V) are members of R), then these observable values will be elements of the relations F, where $i = 1,...,m$.

Propositions of this form are universal in character, and also, to the extent that decision rules have been formulated with reference to empirical facts, they have empirical content. Obviously, a single counter-example suffices to falsify propositions of type A.

However, the economist who uses deductive systems like the previous one in order to analyze causes and consequences in economics and in order to make predictions is not usually ready to discard his model for the sake of a single counter-example[118]. For instance, let us assume that we test a model in the British economy of the 18th century and that we find out that the constitutive statements of this model are not true in the given historical framework. Then the economist who formulated the given model could argue, for instance, that his model was destined for the American economy of the second half of the 20th century, where his model is confirmed.

---

118 At this point, it should be mentioned that K.R. Popper argues that scientists (should) accept with joy, or at least resignation, the refutation of their theories because the refutation of a theory implies that an additional step has been taken away from error (see: K.R. Popper, *The Logic of Scientific Discovery*, New York: Harper & Collins, 1959; Ingvar Johansson, A Critique of Karl Popper's Methodology, Stockholm: Scandinavian University Books, 1975). However, as M. Nicholson has pointed out, the attitude of Popper and the Popperians "is psychologically implausible as well as being of dubious rationality"; see: Nicholson, *Causes and Consequences in International Relations*, p. 70.

However, if someone asked this economist to define the economy for which his model is destined in the abstract, most probably he would not receive an exact answer.

Propositions of type A can be accepted only if they are endowed with a determination of the relevant historical framework. Thus, Propositions of type A must be transformed into Propositions of type B, which are defined as follows:

Proposition of type B: Let W_k be the class of all observations whose result is the identification of the kth historical framework (the kth historical framework is the kth subset of the set of all possible states of the world). The observations w on the states of the world must take place simultaneously with but independently from the observations h on the n-tuple V. Therefore, a proposition of type B states the following: for every observation, w, on the historical framework, for every observation, h, on the n-tuple V, and for every V, *if* the observations on the historical framework identify the kth historical framework (i.e., W_k) and *if* the observations w on the historical framework take place simultaneously with but independently from the observations h on V, *then*, given that the observations h on V satisfy the rule R, V satisfies the relations F_i, where i = 1,...,m.

The fundamental difference between a proposition of type A and a proposition of type B is that the latter is endowed with a determination of the historical framework in which it is applicable. A proposition of type A declares that the observable values of V satisfy the relations F_i, where i = 1,...,m, independently of the corresponding historical framework. On the other hand, a proposition of type B declares that the observable values of V satisfy the relations F_i, where i = 1,...,m, under the condition that the observations on V take place in the kth historical framework. However, usually, the economist cannot completely characterize the relevant historical framework beforehand. Therefore, the first part (i.e., the 'if'-part) of every proposition of type B contains terms that are only partially interpreted.

Let us assume that, in some particular state of the world, the observable values of V satisfy the relations F_i, where $i = 1,...,m$. Then the second part (the 'then') of the basic implication of a proposition of type B is confirmed. If the conclusion of the given implication is true, then the whole proposition is true, independently of the truth value of the first part (the 'if') of the given implication, and, in this case, the whole proposition is confirmed. On the other hand, let us assume that the conclusion of the basic implication of a proposition of type B is not confirmed, i.e., that the observable values of V do not satisfy the relations F_i, where $i = 1,...,m$. In this case, the truth value of the whole proposition depends on the truth value of its first part (the 'if'). But the terms of the first part of the given proposition are not fully interpreted beforehand, and, therefore, we cannot decide if the whole proposition is true or false. Hence, propositions of type B can be confirmed by recourse to empirical data but they cannot be empirically falsified because the terms of the first part of the basic implication of a proposition of type B remain uninterpreted.

By the term 'model', I mean a deductive system whose constitutive statements can be confirmed but they cannot be falsified. A 'theory' can be formulated in terms of propositions of type A or in terms of propositions of type B. If a theory is formulated in terms of propositions of type A, then it is supposed to be confirmed in every possible state of the world. If a theory is formulated in terms of propositions of type B, then the first part (the 'if') of its basic implication must be fully interpreted, because, otherwise, it is a model and not a theory.

Economic models explain economic behavior within the historical frameworks in which they are confirmed, but they cannot be used as prediction devices because the conditions under which they are applicable cannot be determined beforehand. This, however, does not mean that economists should give up the effort to make predictions. It means that predictions that are based on models depend on the subjective judgments made by the economist who is about to make a prediction. For instance, if an economist has to make a prediction about the impact of a specific tax measure on income or unemployment during the next four years, then he must choose the model in terms of which the prediction will take place and which, according to his judgment, has the highest probability of being confirmed by the observation of the n-tuple V during the next four years. The task of ordering alternative models according to the probability that each one of them has of being confirmed is arduous and intimately related to the state of the mind of the econo- mist who evaluates these models. Furthermore, an economist must always have in his mind that, in human systems in general and in economic systems in particular, generalizations describe conse- quences of the intentionality of human consciousness and do not determine human behavior in the same way that natural laws de- termine the behavior of natural bodies.

Nothing appears or disappears on the philosophical/ scientific horizon overnight. In human thought, jumps are rare, painful and costly. Theories succeed each other by being assimilated in each other, like waves, and each theory contributes to the development of other theories.

Thomas Kuhn has argued that scientists think and work in in- commensurable paradigms. According to Kuhn, there are two dif- ferent modes of scientific change: the period of 'normal science' and the period of 'scientific change'. During a period of normal science, there is a broad consensus on the basics of the scientific discipline and what are cognitively significant questions within it. Thus, during a period of normal science, scientists try to solve problems within a generally agreed and consistent set of principles that influ- ence the way of thinking, the gathering of data and the testing of hypotheses. According to Kuhn's terminology, when a discipline is in such a stage of normal science, the practitioners of the discipline work in a common 'paradigm', which is the scientists' guide. In other words, a paradigm suggests new puzzles and approaches to solving those puzzles, and, additionally, it is the standard by which scientists that work within the given paradigm evaluate a proposed solution to a puzzle[119].

---

119 Thomas Kuhn, *The Structure of Scientific Revolutions*, 2nd edition, Chicago: University of Chicago Press, 1971, pp. 38-39.

However, occasionally there is a 'paradigm change', where a paradigm is replaced by another. According to Kuhn, this type of change is qualitatively different from the change that takes place in normal science. A paradigm change means that the concepts themselves change, i.e., it marks a total reinterpretation of a scientific system. For instance, in Kuhn's view, the conversion from the geocentric to the heliocentric view is a paradigm change. Kuhn argued that the different paradigms are incommensurable and incompatible with each other. Kuhn's principle of incommensurability means that there is no common measure because the methods of comparison and evaluation change during a paradigm change, and, furthermore, the languages of theories from different paradigms may not be inter-translatable. One has to choose among different paradigms, but there appears to be no rational basis for choosing one paradigm over another. Thus, in Kuhn's view, a paradigm change is a jump. Kuhn states:

> [N]ormal (non-revolutionary) science ultimately leads only to the recognition of anomalies and to crises. And these are terminated, not by deliberation and interpretation, but by a relatively sudden and unstructured event like the gestalt switch.[120]

Imre Lakatos took a rather different starting point. He used the term 'research program'[121] instead of the term 'paradigm'. According to Lakatos, a research program consists of: a 'hard core' (i.e., a base theory that uniquely defines the identity of the given research program and is protected by all theories that belong to the same research program), the 'protective belt' (the features that may be altered), the 'negative heuristic' (which defines what should not be researched — namely, the hard core) and the 'positive heuristic' (which defines what should be researched). Michael Nicholson has explained Lakatos's concept of a research program as follows:

> A theory which is shown to be inadequate is replaced by one which is rather better but typically by one which is of the same family...We have a sequence of theories, T(1), T(2), T(3) and so on, each of which explains more than its predecessor and thus

120 Ibid., p. 122.
121 Imre Lakatos, "Falsification and Methodology of Scientific Research Programmes", in I. Lakatos and A. Musgrave (eds), *Criticism and the Growth of Knowledge*, Cambridge: Cambridge University Press, 1970.

supersedes it. This sequence of theories is known as a scientific research program. The family relationship is carried on by the 'negative heuristic' or 'hard core' of propositions which will not be doubted, at least during the course of the research program. In general it is not to be supposed that all observations will fit neatly into this framework and objections will not be raised. The response is not to abandon the hard-core assumptions but to defend them by means of *ad hoc* or 'auxiliary' hypotheses which will protect the core against recalcitrant facts. These auxiliary hypotheses are expendable and will be abandoned or modified if new observations require it. However, they will always be modified in such a way as to defend the hard core of the research program.[122]

Lakatos argues that alterations to the protective belt are not always equal. If an alteration expands the explanatory power of the corresponding research program, then the alteration is said to be 'progressive'. If an alteration is merely an *ad hoc* maneuver in order to fix a problem and does not add to the explanatory domain of the theory, then it is said to be 'degenerate'. In Lakatos's view, a research program is 'progressive' to the extent that a sufficient number of the alterations to its protective belt are progressive. On the other hand, a research program is 'degenerate' when the alterations to its protective belt "explain only those particular facts they were called in to explain and otherwise add nothing to the theory beyond this"[123]. Thus, "the research program sinks, so to speak, under the weight of its *ad hoc* hypotheses"[124]. In contrast to Kuhn's principle of incommensurability, Lakatos argues that "it is normal for the scientific community in any particular area to be following more than one research program at the same time", and that "in the competition between research programs...a degenerate program slowly gives way to a progressive program"[125]. Therefore, Lakatos's concept of research programs provides what he calls a rational reconstruction of what goes on in a developing scientific discipline, and it provides a criterion for selection between research programs. But Lakatos's criterion is not clear-cut.

---

122 Nicholson, *Causes and Consequences in International Relations*, pp. 72-73.
123 Ibid., p. 74.
124 Ibid., p. 74.
125 Ibid., pp. 73-74.

Lakatos was right in criticizing Kuhn's principle of incommensurability. For instance, let us consider Euclidean geometry and non-Euclidean geometries. The essential difference between Euclidean geometry and non-Euclidean geometries is the nature of parallel lines. In the first book of Euclid's *Elements*, we read that "parallel straight lines are straight lines which, being in the same plane and being produced indefinitely in both directions, do not meet one another in both directions". According to Euclid's fifth postulate (known also as 'Euclid's parallel postulate'), "if a straight line falling on two straight lines make the interior angles on the same side less than two right angles, the two straight lines, if produced indefinitely, meet on that side on which are the angles less than the two right angles". Let us assume that two straight lines, A and B, indefinitely extended in a two-dimensional plane, are both perpendicular to a third line, C. Then the differences between Euclidean geometry on the one hand and non-Euclidean geometries on the other hand can be defined as follows: In Euclidean geometry, according to Euclid's parallel postulate, the lines A and B remain at a constant distance from each other even if extended to infinity. In hyperbolic geometry[126], the lines A and B 'curve away' from each other, and, therefore, the distance between A and B increases as one moves further from the points of intersection with the common perpendicular C. In elliptic geometry[127], the lines A and B 'curve toward' each other and eventually intersect. The axiomatic systems of Euclidean geometry, hyperbolic geometry and elliptic geometry are different from each other, and, therefore, they can be considered

---

126 Hyperbolic geometry was methodically studied by in the 19th century by János Bolyai and Nikolai Ivanovich Lobachevsky, after whom it sometimes is named. The term 'hyperbolic geometry' was introduced by Felix Klein in 1871. Einstein applied hyperbolic geometry in his theory of general relativity, according to which space and time are shaped into curves determined by matter and energy and the curvature of space controls the movement of matter within it. Einstein's theory of general relativity implies that the geometry of the universe is a hyperbolic one.

127 Elliptic geometry was put in a rigorous mathematical setting in the 19th century by Bertrand Riemann. One can easily understand elliptic geometry if he looks at a globe. Neighboring lines of longitude appear to be parallel at the equator, but they intersect at the poles.

as Kuhnian paradigms. However, in contrast to Kuhn's theory, they are not incommensurable, and, in fact, they are equiconsistent. In 1868, Eugenio Beltrami proved that Euclidean geometry and hyperbolic geometry were equiconsistent, so that hyperbolic geometry was logically consistent if and only if Euclidean geometry was. In general, non-Euclidean geometries are consistent if and only if Euclidean geometry is consistent:

> The work of Felix Klein (1849–1925) was highly influential in bringing all of the geometries together under one umbrella. He first showed that it was possible to consider both Euclidean and non-Euclidean geometries as special cases of a projective surface. This led to an important corollary, namely, that non-Euclidean geometry is consistent if and only if Euclidean geometry is consistent.[128]

If the three previous paradigms — namely, Euclidean geometry, hyperbolic geometry and elliptic geometry — had been totally and generally incommensurable, there would be no rational reasons for choosing any of them. However, there are rational reasons for choosing the appropriate geometric paradigm on different occasions. Euclidean geometry is an excellent theory for the study of the 'local' structure of the globe. For instance, we should apply Euclidean geometry in order to compute the area of a farm or a house. But, if we want to study the 'global' structure of the globe, then we need elliptic geometry. In fact, spherical geometry, which describes the surface of the sphere, is used by pilots and ship captains as they navigate around the world. The sum of the angles of 'small' triangles, like the triangles drawn on a football field, is infinitely close to 180 degrees, whereas the sum of the angles of 'big' triangles, like the triangle whose vertices are New York, Los Angeles and Tampa, is more than 180 degrees. Moreover, if matter and energy distort space and if the distortions of space affect the motions of matter and energy, then, as Albert Einstein has argued, the correct geometry of our universe will be hyperbolic geometry. Therefore, given that there are rational reasons for choosing the appropriate geometric paradigm on different occasions, the different geometric paradigms

---

128 Nathalie Sinclair, *The History of the Geometry Curriculum in the United States*, Information Age Publishing, Inc., 2008, p. 24.

are commensurable and Kuhn's principle of incommensurability is wrong. From this viewpoint, Lakatos seems to be right. However, Lakatos's view is not absolutely correct, because all of the different geometric paradigms (or rather 'research programs') are true and equiconsistent, and their explanatory power depends on the geometric framework in which one works each time. In fact, contra Lakatos and the Lakatosians, different research programs are not necessarily competitive with each other, but they can be complementary to each other.

Lakatos identified the defects of the mechanistic character of the classical picture of science, and he attempted to cure them by proposing the methodology of scientific research programs as "a way of incorporating the dynamics of change into the classical picture of science as essentially a rational and cumulative advance of knowledge"[129]. Thus, Lakatos avoided the mistakes of Kuhn, who stressed the incommensurability of paradigms and the structural stability of the 'normal' practise of science, but Lakatos's dynamic epistemology cannot account for the nonlinear character and the complexity of the dialectical process according to which knowledge develops. Complexity studies give rise to what Silvio Fontowicz and Jerry Ravetz have called 'postnormal science', which "accepts the legitimacy of different perspectives from all those stakeholders around the table"[130]. In fact, postnormal science "does not seek to overthrow the fundamentals of the traditional sciences which came before it; rather it seeks to have its roots in the experience of uncertainty, impermanence, ambiguity and non-determinism"[131].

Like every other creative activity, philosophical thought — which is the most general form of the human being's intellectual activity — is a continuous and unstoppable life-long struggle. In other words, philosophy is primarily a disposition for a methodical search for truth; only secondarily is it an accomplished search.

---

129 Nicholson, *Causes and Consequences in International Relations*, p. 78.
130 Silvio Fontowicz and Jerry Ravetz quoted in: Ziauddin Sardar and Iwona Abrams, *Introducing Chaos*, Cambridge: Icon Books, 1999.
131 See: Nick Obolensky, *Complex Adaptive Leadership: Embracing Paradox and Uncertainty*, Burlington: Gower Publishing, 2010, p. 89.

Philosophical (and scientific) knowledge develops according to the following dialectical process: a theory is formulated in response to another theory; elements of the new theory are somehow connected with elements of the previous theory; in the sequel, the new theory undergoes various types of transformation, expansion and development, or it undergoes some kind of condensation, or even it may temporarily disappear before it reappears adequately renewed. For instance, the philosophy of the sophists influenced the skepticism of the 'New Academy'[132]; the Neo-Platonism of Proclus, especially in its Christianized version, which is due to Dionysius the Areopagite, influenced Hegelianism; the ancient concept of 'kairos' became the focal point of various types of kairological studies in modern philosophy and psychoanalysis, etc[133].

---

132 Around 266 BC, Arcesilaus became head of the Platonic Academy, and adopted skepticism as a central tenet of Platonism. This skeptical period of Platonism, from Arcesilaus to Philo of Larissa (154/3-84/3 BC), is known as the 'New Academy'.

133 See: Evangelos Moutsopoulos, *He Poreia tou Pneumatos: He Axie* (The Itinerary of Spirit: Values), Athens: 1977, in Greek; Evangelos Moutsopoulos, *Kairos et alternance: d' Empédocle à Platon*, Athènes: Académie d' Athènes, 1989.

Chapter 8. Formal Methods Of Analysis In Economics

By 'formal methods', I mean the use of logic and mathematics to build models of economic systems or situations. The deductive structure of a model helps one to explore the consequences of alternative assumptions. This contrasts, for example, with the use of statistical methods solely for the purpose of summarizing empirical data. One can experiment with the model (by changing the assumptions) when it would be impossible or too dangerous to experiment with the world of experience. The most common formal methods in economics are: Linear Programing, Decision Theory, Game Theory and its extensions, and Artificial Intelligence.

In mathematics and computer science, 'optimization' refers to the selection of an 'optimal' element from some set of available alternatives. In other words, this means solving problems in which one seeks to minimize or maximize a function by systematically choosing the values of variables from within an allowed set. Pierre de Fermat (17th century) and Joseph-Louis Lagrange (1736–1813) found calculus-based formulas for computing optima (minima and maxima), and Isaac Newton (1643–1727) and Friedrich Gauss (1777–1855) developed iterative methods for approximating an op-

timum. Historically, the first term for optimization is 'linear programing', which is a method for finding the minimum or maximum
value of a linear function subject to various constraints in the form
of linear inequalities. The first contributions to linear programing
are due to the Soviet mathematician and economist Leonid Vitali-
yevich Kantorovich (1912–1986), who won the Nobel Prize in Economics in 1975. In 1947, the American mathematician George B.
Dantzig[134] formulated and published the simplex method for solving linear-programming problems, and he has been recognized as the
founder of modern linear programming. Linear Programming has many
applications in economics and management[135].

However, the original models of linear programing were focused on deliberate choices made by parties involved. As it has
been pointed out by L.F. Richardson[136], for instance, such models
describe "what would happen if people did not stop to think". In
other words, the models of linear programing are concerned with
decision makers who are weighing up the possible consequences
of alternative actions and policies; these are often called 'rational
actor' models. As I shall explain in Chapter 9, these models can be
developed to take account of multiple objectives or differences in
perception by expressing the actors' motivations in terms of preferences for different possible outcomes. But theories based on preferences have an important defect: they over-concentrate on actors'
wants or interests at the expense of attention to needs[137]. Roger A.
Coate and Jerel A. Rosati argue that:

> human needs are a powerful source of explanation of human
> behavior and social interaction. All individuals have needs that
> they strive to satisfy, either by using the system, 'acting on the

---

134 G.B. Dantzig, *Linear Programming and Extensions*, Princeton, NJ:
Princeton University Press, 1963.

135 See: J.K. Strayer, *Linear Programming and Its Applications*, New York:
Springer-Verlag, 1989.

136 L.F. Richardson, "Generalized Foreign Politics: A Study in Group
Psychology", in O.M. Ashford, H. Charnock et al. (eds), *Collected
Papers of Lewis Fry Richardson, Vol. 2: Quantitative Psychology and Studies
of Conflict*, Cambridge: Cambridge University Press, 1993, pp. 261-350.

137 John Burton, *Resolving Deep-Rooted Conflicts*, Lanham: University Press
of America, 1987, chapter 5.

---

fringes', or acting as a reformist or revolutionary. Given this condition, social systems must be responsive to individual needs,
or be subject to instability and forced change (possibly through
violence or conflict).[138]

The psychologist Abraham Maslow[139] has argued that humans
need a number of essentials to survive, and these essentials include both physical and non-physical elements needed for human
growth and development as well as those things that human beings are innately driven to attain. Maslow's needs pyramid starts
with the physiological needs, and these are followed by the need for
safety, then belonging/ love, esteem and, finally, self-actualization.
However, other needs theorists perceive human needs in a different
way — namely, as an emergent collection of human development
essentials — and they argue that needs do not have a hierarchical
order, but needs are sought simultaneously in an intense and relent-
less manner[140]. In general, needs theorists have helped economists
identify the significance of human needs in economic analysis, since
economic action and particularly economic competition are closely
related to actors' unyielding drive to meet their unmet needs on the
individual, group and societal levels.

The earliest and simplest formal models of choice were developed by researchers working within the framework of Decision
Theory. Decision Theory is concerned with the analysis of choices
available to an actor who is unsure about the consequences of each
possible option. Usually, uncertainty is expressed by a probability,
and the model demands that the actor should be able to measure
the desirability or the undesirability — namely, the 'utility' — of
each possible outcome. In the sequel, one can compute the expected
utility of each available option by multiplying the utilities of the
possible outcomes by their probabilities once that option is chosen.

---

138 R.A. Coate and J.A. Rosati, "Preface", in R.A. Coate and J.A. Rosati
(eds), *The Power of Human Needs in World Society*, Boulder, Colorado:
Lynn Rienner, 1988.

139 A.H. Maslow, "A Theory of Human Motivation", *Psychological Review*,
Vol. 50, 1943, pp. 370-396.

140 See: Jay Rothman, *Resolving Identity-Based Conflict in Nations,
Organizations, and Communities*, San Francisco, CA: Jossey-Bass
Publishers, 1997.

Two very common criteria of 'rational choice' are then to choose the option whose best gain is better than the best gain of all other available options (this is the optimistic, or aggressive, decision-making rule, known as 'maximax criterion') or to choose the option whose worst loss is better than the least loss of all other available options (this is the pessimistic, or conservative, decision-making rule, known as 'maximin criterion'). In Decision Theory, there are several defensible decision criteria, and some of them do not require the probabilities of events to be known. Furthermore, it is widely recognized that, usually, different outcomes will be better for different reasons. In other words, usually, the attractiveness of an outcome will not depend on just one factor (not even profit[141]). Thus, several forms of multiple criteria analysis have been developed in order to model how different advantages are weighed up against

---

141 Many economists assume that the profit-maximization assumption rests on the same universal grounds as the assumption of utility-index maximization (rationality). Profit maximization implies rationality, but rationality is consistent with other things as well as profits. Profit is just one among many related goals sought by the firm. Thus, the profit-maximization assumption should be replaced by the more general assumption of preference-function maximization; see: Benjamin Higgins, "Elements of Indeterminacy in the Theory of Non-Perfect Competition", *American Economic Review*, Vol. 29, 1939, pp. 468-479. Higgins has argued that profit maximization is a survival condition in perfect competition, but its force is much weaker in the case of imperfect competition, since, under such conditions, the entrepreneur may be expected to have margins with which to work and with which to satisfy other than the desire for profit. Higgins has classified the desires that lead to non-profit-maximization equilibria into three categories: (i) leisure leads the entrepreneur to produce at a point below the profit-maximizing output; (ii) desire to own a large firm, power and prestige leads the entrepreneur to produce at a level above the profit-maximizing output; (iii) commitment to a 'just-price' idea or reluctance to experiment leads the entrepreneur to sustain the status quo, whether he is producing an output above or below the profit-maximizing output. Thus, Higgins has introduced indifference curves (relating profit to output) into the standard dollars-output diagram, so that tangency of the net-profits curve to an indifference curve maximizes the entrepreneur's utility index.

each other[142]. Moreover, Herbert Simon developed the concept of 'bounded rationality'[143]. According to this, often decision-makers do not explore all alternatives to find the optimal one, but they look only until they find something good enough. However, the proposals by Simon as well as by John Dewey[144], O.G. Brim[145] and others are all 'sequential', in the sense that they divide decision processes into parts that always come in the same sequence. Eberhard Witte has criticized the idea that the decision process can, generally speaking, be divided into consecutive 'stages'. According to Witte, the 'stages' are performed in parallel rather than in sequence: "human beings cannot gather information without in some way simultaneously developing alternatives...This is a package of operations and the succession of these packages over time constitutes the total decision-making process"[146].

Despite its progress, Decision Theory has two basic defects: (i) Decision Theory is based on a fixed universe of possibilities, and, therefore, it considers the 'known unknowns' but not the 'unknown unknowns', i.e., significant events may be 'outside the model'. This line of argument, known as the "ludic fallacy"[147], stresses that we must always be aware of the limits of formal models. (ii) Decision Theory is concerned only with a single decision-maker or a group already engaged in collective action, whereas much of economics

---

142 See: Valerie Belton, "Multiple Criteria Decision Analysis: Practically the Only Way to Choose", in L.C. Hendry and R.W. Engelese (eds), *OR Tutorial Papers*, Birmingham: Operational Research Society, 1990.

143 H.A. Simon, *Reason in Human Affairs*, Oxford: Basil Blackwell and Stanford: Stanford University Press, 1983.

144 John Dewey, *How We Think*, in *Middle Works*, Vol. 6, 1978 (originally published in 1910), pp. 177-356.

145 O.G. Brim et al., *Personality and Decision Processes: Studies in the Social Psychology of Thinking*, Stanford: Stanford University Press, 1962.

146 Eberhard Witte, "Field Research on Complex Decision-Making Processes: The Phase Theorem", *International Studies of Management and Organization*, Vol. 2, 1972, p. 180.

147 The term "ludic fallacy" is a term coined by Nassim Nicholas Taleb. It is from the Latin 'ludus', meaning, 'play', 'game', and it refers to "the misuse of games to model real-life situations"; see: N.N. Taleb, *The Black Swan: The Impact of the Highly Improbable*, New York: Random House, 2007.

and politics concerns the interplay between decisions made separately, by independent actors, but which affect each other. This is the domain of Game Theory.

Game Theory was developed from early work on Decision Theory in order to "analyze the way that two or more *players* or parties choose actions or strategies that jointly affect each participant"[148]. This theory was largely developed by the mathematician John von Neumann (1903–1957). However, the history of the subject shows that, before von Neumann's superlative 1928 paper "Theory of Parlor Games", the great French analyst Émil Borel (1871–1956) had also attempted to mathematicize the concept of strategy, and also the research work of Abraham Wald (1902–1950) in the theory of 'statistical decision functions' was intimately related to game theory. Samuelson and Nordhaus have summarized the basic concepts of game theory as follows:

> The basic structure of a game includes the players, who have different actions or strategies; and the payoffs, which describe the profits or other benefits that the players obtain in each outcome. The key new concept is the payoff table of a game, which shows the strategies and the payoffs or profits of the different players. The key to choosing strategies in game theory is for players to think through both their own and their opponent's goals, never forgetting that the other side is doing the same. When playing a game in economics or any other field, assume that your opponents will choose their best options. Then pick your strategy so as to maximize your benefit, always assuming that your opponent is similarly analyzing your options. Sometimes a dominant strategy is available, one that is best no matter what the opposition does. More often, we find the Nash equilibrium (or noncooperative equilibrium) most useful. A Nash equilibrium is one in which no player can improve his or her payoff given the other player's strategy. Sometimes, parties can collude or cooperate, which produces the cooperative equilibrium.[149]

A significant part of advanced game-theoretical research works emphasizes various forms of dynamic analysis. Within a given game, analysis concentrates on the modification of strategies as the game unfolds, instead of assuming that strategies are chosen once-and-for-all. Moreover, multi-level games consider series of linked

---

148 Samuelson and Nordhaus, *Economics*, p. 205.
149 Ibid., p. 212.

games and, within the framework of a multi-level game, the out-come of each stage determines which game is to be played next[150]. Hypergame[151] analysis goes further by starting from the assumption that the players may perceive the game in quite different terms. The basic model of hypergame analysis is not a single game per-ceived by all the players but a set of subjective games, each express-ing one player's view of the situation. Thus, in hypergame terms, a situation in which both players correctly perceive the same game is said to be a level-zero hypergame; a situation in which both play-ers believe they are playing the same game while at least one player misperceives the game is said to be a level-one hypergame; a situ-ation in which at least one perceives the other player's (assumed) misperceptions is said to be a level-two hypergame. The analysis of hypergames of level higher than two is a very arduous task, be-cause these hypergames require long mental recursions of the type 'I think he thinks I think he thinks, and so on'.

Despite its progress, Game Theory has two basic defects: (i) Even though many game-theoretical models are endowed with a set of definite assumptions, they still cannot make strong predictions about the outcome to be expected. In fact, they may lead to useful predictions about the players' tactical behavior, but they usually cannot predict whose tactics are likely to succeed. In Game Theory, as well as in other methods used in (neo)classical microeconom-ics (e.g. indifference-curve analysis and marginal-utility analysis), the actor is usually an ideal type formulated to fit his prescribed role in equilibrium theory. Thus, for instance, C. Reynolds[152], P.A.

---

150 See for instance: Yianis Varoufakis, *Rational Conflict*, Oxford: Blackwell, 1991.

151 See: P.G. Bennett and M.R. Dando, "Complex Strategic Analysis: A Study of the Fall of France", *Journal of Operational Research Society*, Vol. 33, 1979, pp. 41-50; M.A. Takahashi, N.M. Fraser and K.W. Hipel, "A Procedure for Analyzing Hypergames", *European Journal of Operational Research*, Vol. 18, 1984, pp. 111–122.

152 Charles Reynolds, "Deterrence", *Review of International Studies*, Vol. 15, 1989, pp. 67-74.

Schrodt[153] and N.N. Taleb[154] provide important warnings. (ii) Most game-theoretical models, following the epistemological legacy of classical political economy, treat the relevant players (e.g. nations, firms, households, etc.) as homogeneous units ('unitary actors'). However, every collective actor (e.g. a national government, the executive apparatus of a firm, etc.) is subject to internal games (between bureaucracies, key individuals and the like), and, therefore, every collective player is a game and should not be treated as a homogeneous unit. Thus, if every player is a game, the formulation of multi-level game-theoretical models is much more complicated than most game theorists assume. For this reason, P.G. Bennett, A. Tait and K. Macdonagh[155] have proposed that multi-level game-theoretical models must include a detailed description of the problem-structuring method that they have followed, explaining the linkage of issues at different levels.

Another approach to the use of formal methods in economics is based on Artificial Intelligence[156] (AI). AI refers to attempts to build computer systems that simulate human reasoning. There are several applications of AI techniques in finance, business and economic analysis[157], especially because AI extends the capabilities of computers and therefore helps economists and managers process complex databases more efficiently. However, due to Kurt Gödel's theorems[158], the total formalization of knowledge is impossible. Fur-

---

153 P.A. Schrodt, "Adaptive Precedent-Based Logic and Rational Choice; a Comparison of Two Approaches to the Modelling of International Behavior", in U. Luterbacher and M.D. Ward (eds), *Dynamic Models of International Conflict*, Boulder: Lynne Reinner, 1985, pp. 373-400.

154 Taleb, *The Black Swan*.

155 Peter Bennett, Andrew Tait and Kieran Macdonagh, "INTERACT: Developing Software for Interactive Decisions", *Group Decision and Negotiation*, Vol. 3, 1994, pp. 351-372.

156 For a general introduction, see: Joseph Weizenbaum, *Computer Power and Human Reason: From Judgment to Calculation*, London: Penguin, 1984.

157 See for instance: Phillip Ein-Dor (ed.), *Artificial Intelligence in Economics and Management*, Dordrecht: Kluwer Academic Publishers, 1996.

158 Gödel's incompleteness theorem of 1931 proved that, within any logically consistent system for mathematics, there will be some statements about numbers that are true but that can never be proved. In general, Kleene has summarized and explained the results of Gödel's research

thermore, John von Neumann[159] has stressed the rule-bound inflexibility or "brittleness" of machine behavior: the fact that machines are susceptible to cataclysmic "crashes" due to slight causes (e.g. slight hardware malfunctions, software glitches and 'bad data') is related to the formal, or rule-bound, character of machine behavior, i.e., to the fact that machines need "rules of conduct to cover every eventuality"[160]. In contrast to machine behavior, human behavior is less formal and more flexible. Following these arguments, Hubert Dreyfus has stressed that a range of high-level human behavior cannot be algorithmically specified: the "immediate intuitive situational response that is characteristic of [human] expertise" depends "almost entirely on intuition and hardly at all on analysis and comparison of alternatives"[161].

Alexander Rosenberg[162] has studied the use of formal methods in economics, and he has argued that economics have succeeded in producing only formal mathematical systems without empirical relevance. According to Rosenberg, there is a stronger similarity between the cognitive status of economics and Euclidean geometry rather than between economics and classical physics or evolutionary biology, in the sense that 'economic theory' is a set of abstract

---

work as follows: "Any effectively generated theory capable of expressing elementary arithmetic cannot be both consistent and complete. In particular, for any consistent, effectively generated formal theory that proves certain basic arithmetic truths, there is an arithmetical statement that is true but not provable in the theory" (S.C. Kleene, *Mathematical Logic*, London: Dover, 2002, p. 250).

159 John von Neumann, *First Draft of a Report to the EDVAC*, Moore School of Engineering, University of Pennsylvania, June 30, 1945.

160 Alan Turing, "Computing Machinery and Intelligence", *Mind*, Vol. LIX, 1950, pp. 433-460.

161 H.L. Dreyfus, "Intelligence Without Representation: Merleau-Ponty's Critique of Mental Representation", *Phenomenology and the Cognitive Sciences*, Vol. 1, 2002, pp. 367-383; H.L. Dreyfus and S.E. Dreyfus, *Mind Over Machine: The Power of Human Intuition and Expertise in the Age of the Computer*, Oxford: Basil Blackwell, 1986; H.L. Dreyfus, *What Computers Still Can't Do*, Cambridge, MA: M.I.T. Press, 1992.

162 Alexander Rosenberg, *Economics: Mathematical Politics or Science of Diminishing Returns?*, Chicago: University of Chicago Press, 1992, Chapter 8.

and non-empirical axioms and the exercise of 'doing economics' consists in deriving theorems from these axioms. Furthermore, Rosenberg argues that this is not a satisfactory way of understanding the intellectual program of economics and that the intellectual charge for the academic discipline of economics is to provide social-scientific basis for understanding, explaining and perhaps predicting economic phenomena.

CHAPTER 9. RATIONALITY AND ECONOMICS: FROM RATIONALITY TO KAIRICITY

A genealogy of ratio

Rationality is attributed to 'Homo Sapiens' in virtue of the ability to reason and act upon the consequences of deliberation. The concept of rationality requires for its elucidation reference to the concept of reason. The terms reason and rationality are derived from the Latin term 'ratio'. In certain conceptual communities, rational and reasonable could be used interchangeably.

In the context of classical Greek philosophy, cognition does not produce knowledge by itself, but it is viewed as a process whereby the mind receives and processes sense-data. In particular, in Plato's *Timaeus*, 45d, the soul, like the body, is characterized by "that sensation which we now term 'seeing'"; and, in Aristotle's *On Sense and the Sensible*, 438b10, the soul operates as the center of sensation. Even though, for Plato, cognition is not based on bodily sensations, Plato argues that cognition is based on a peculiar mental *sensation*. In particular, according to Plato, the mind does not reproduce an external object through conceptualization, nor does it create mental models of an external object, but it *participates* in the transcendental idea of an external object, and, therefore, it knows an external object due to the *experience* of the light of the corresponding idea. Therefore, Plato's notion of reason is the synthesis of logic and experience.

On the other hand, in the Middle Ages, Thomas Aquinas and generally the scholastics ignored that, when Plato created the term idea, he simultaneously stressed that vision is the most representative sense of human mental life. Thus, the medieval West ignored that, in the context of Plato's philosophy, knowledge, i.e., consciousness's relationship with truth, is primarily a spiritual *experience*, and, for this reason, it primarily consists in a psychological state and only secondarily in the discovery of causal relations (logical accountability). As Plato himself argues in his *Theaetetus*, 184d, the unity of the 'idea' as vision makes psychological unity possible:

> Yes, for it would be strange indeed, my boy, if there are many senses ensconced within us, as if we were so many wooden horses of Troy, and they do not all unite in one power, whether we should call it soul or something else, by which we perceive through these as instruments the objects of perception....Now the reason why I am so precise about the matter is this: I want to know whether there is some one and the same power within ourselves by which we perceive black and white through the eyes, and again other qualities...

Hence, in contrast to the Greek philosophical tradition, the scholastics interpreted Plato's 'ideas' as logically self-subsistent entities. But the classical Greek philosophers never exhausted rationality in logical consistence.

When the West became aware that the identification of reason with logic and hence the distinction between reason and experience are problematic and extremely restrictive conditions, it stopped using the terms 'rational' and 'reasonable' interchangeably. Thus, in the context of modern Western thought, 'rationality' implies logical coercion, whereas, according to the *Oxford English Dictionary*, 'reasonableness' is seen as a more social virtue than rationality, and it is defined as follows: "Having sound judgment; sensible, sane, in which it is noted to be equivalent to a sense of 'rational' and also "not asking too much". From the previous connection between the modern notion of reasonableness and the traditional Western way of understanding rationality as logical necessity/ consistence, it follows that, in conflicts about the terms of social co-operation, willingness to listen to the reasons offered by others consists in an openness to their perspectives and interests and not in conformity to something that is deemed logically self-subsistent. In other words, in the classical Greek philosophical context, rationality and reasonableness can be used interchangeably, since, for the classical Greek philosophers, reason consists of both logic and experience, whereas, in the context of modern Western thought, rationality is equated with logical necessity/consistence and 'reasonableness' is equated with the disposition to act on reasons of all kinds.

As a result of the West's restrictive definition of rationality and the distinction between 'rationality' and reasonableness' within the context of modern Western thought, the notion of rationality has given rise to several disputes — such as the following: how irrational people actually are and what the implications of human deficiencies in analytical data processing are for policy-making[163]; how far rationality has to be assumed in interpreting any culture[164]; whether rational choice theory is the best research program in the social sciences[165]; how far the concept of rationality can usefully be extended from individual human beings to societies[166].

Rationality and the 'Homo Economicus' in modern economic thought

According to earlier, defunct formulations of the concept of rationality, on which classical economics is based, the 'Homo Economicus' ('Economic Man') is an approximation or model of 'Homo Sapiens'. The term 'Economic Man' was used for the first time in the late 19th century by critics of John Stuart Mill's work on political

163 P. Slovik, B. Fischhoff and S. Lichtenstein, "Regulations of Risk: A Psychological Perspective", in R.G. Noll (ed.), *Regulatory Policy in the Social Sciences*, Berkeley: University of California Press, 1985.

164 M. Hollis and S. Lukes (eds), *Rationality and Relativism*, Cambridge, Mass.: MIT Press, 1979.

165 S.L. Popkin, *The Rational Peasant: the Political Economy of Rural Society in Vietnam*, Berkeley: University of California Press, 1979.

166 B. Barry and R. Hardin (eds), *Rational Man and Irrational Society?* — *An Introduction and Sourcebook*, Beverly Hills, Calif.: Sage, 1982.

economy[167]. According to John Stuart Mill, political economy "does not treat the whole of man's nature as modified by the social state, nor of the whole conduct of man in society. It is concerned with him solely as a being who desires to possess wealth, and who is capable of judging the comparative efficacy of means for obtaining that end"[168]. Additionally, in the same work, John Stuart Mill goes on to write that he is proposing "an arbitrary definition of man, as a being who inevitably does that by which he may obtain the greatest amount of necessaries, conveniences, and luxuries, with the smallest quantity of labour and physical self-denial with which they can be obtained".

Before John Stuart Mill, the 'Economic Man' had been postulated by Adam Smith and David Ricardo. In the *Wealth of Nations*, Adam Smith wrote: "It is not from the benevolence of the butcher, the brewer, or the baker that we expect our dinner, but from their regard to their own interest"[169].

In the 19th century, many economists — such as Francis Edgeworth, William Stanley Jevons, Léon Walras and Vilfredo Pareto — formulated mathematical models based on the postulate of the 'Economic Man'. Moreover, in the 20th century, Lionel Robbins's rational choice theory dominated mainstream economics. Within the framework of Lionel Robbins's rational choice theory, the term 'Economic Man' refers to a person who acts in a logically consistent manner on complete knowledge out of self-interest and desire for economic wealth.

'Homo Economicus' is seen as 'rational' in the sense that his well-being is defined by a well-ordered set of goals or preferences and he acts efficiently in order to pursue his goals and thus opti-

---

167 See: Joseph Persky, "Retrospectives: The Ethology of Homo Economicus", *The Journal of Economic Perspectives*, Vol. 9, 1995, pp. 221-231.

168 J.S. Mill, *Essays on Some Unsettled Questions of Political Economy*, 2nd edition, London: Longmans, Green Reader & Dyer, 1874, essay 5, paragraphs 38 and 48.

169 Adam Smith, *The Wealth of Nations*, New York: Penguin Classics, 1986 (originally published in 1776), p. 119.

mize his individual utility function. The 'Homo Economicus' assumptions have been criticized on the following grounds:

(i) Economic anthropologists, such as Marshall Sahlins[170], Karl Polanyi[171] and Maurice Godelier[172], have shown that, in traditional societies, people make economic decisions (about production and exchange of goods) by following patterns of reciprocity that are very different from the assumptions of the 'Homo Economicus' model. Such systems are known as 'gift economy' rather than market economy, and they express the economic ethos of several traditional societies[173] as well as of great religious cultures[174].

(ii) Many economists, such as Thorstein Veblen, John Maynard Keynes, Herbert Simon as well as many of the 'Austrian School', ar-

---

170 Marshall Sahlins, *Stone Age Economics*, 2nd revised edition, London: Routledge, 2003.

171 Karl Polanyi, *The Great Transformation*, Boston: Beacon Press, 2001.

172 Maurice Godelier, *The Enigma of the Gift*, Chicago: University of Chicago Press, 1999.

173 For instance: (i) prior to the 19th century, Pacific Island societies were gift economies; (ii) in Papua New Guinea, gift economy structures (e.g. 'Kula ring' and 'Moka exchange') survived in the 20th century; (iii) in the Sierra Tarahumara of North Western Mexico, there is a custom called 'kórima', according to which it is one's duty to share his wealth with anyone; (iv) Native Americans who lived in the Pacific Northwest practiced the 'potlatch' ritual, according to which leaders give away large amounts of goods to their followers, strengthening group relations.

174 In the Christian Bible, we read: "Let no one say when he is tempted, 'I am tempted by God'; for God cannot be tempted with evil and he himself tempts no one; but each person is tempted when he is lured and enticed by his own desire. Then desire, when it has conceived, gives birth to sin; and sin, when it is full-grown, brings forth death" (*James*, 1:13-15). In Judaism, we read: "Envy and desire and ambition drive a man out of the world" (*Mishnah*, Abot 4.28). In Islam, we read: "Have you seen him who makes his desire his god, and God sends him astray purposely, and seals up his hearing and his heart, and sets on his sight a covering? Who, then, will lead him after God [has condemned him]? Will you not then heed?" (*Qur'an*, 45.23). In Hinduism, we read: "There are three gates to self-destructive hell: lust, anger, and greed" (*Bhagavad Gita*, 16.21). In Buddhism, we read: "The man who gathers flowers [of sensual pleasure], whose mind is distracted and who is insatiate in desires, the Destroyer brings under his sway" (*Dhammapada*, 48).

gue that the 'Homo Economicus' model postulates an actor with too great of an understanding of macroeconomics and economic forecasting in his decision-making, and they stress that economic decision-making is characterized by uncertainty and bounded rationality, and not by perfect information.

(iii) In 1995, C.R. Fox and A.N. Tversky[175], two pioneers of cognitive science and behavioral finance, questioned the rationality of investors by showing the tendency of investors to make risk-averse choices in gains and risk-seeking choices in losses. Moreover, investors appeared as very risk-averse for small losses but indifferent for a small chance of a large loss.

(iv) The Swiss economist Bruno Frey has argued that the 'Homo Economicus' model puts too much emphasis on extrinsic motivation (rewards and punishments from the social environment) and underestimates or ignores intrinsic motivation. Therefore, as Bruno Frey, has pointed out, it is impossible to understand how the 'Homo Economicus' would be a hero in war or would get inherent pleasure from craftsmanship. Frey argues that the 'Homo Economicus' model and, in general, the economic models that are based on the 'Homo Economicus' cannot "accurately capture the various notions of happiness and well-being put forward in the literature on the good life"[176].

(v) Rational choice theory often leads us down the path of empirical irrelevance. For instance, Robert Axelrod[177] has conducted empirical research to examine the manner in which and the extent to which real human reasoners deal with prisoners' dilemmas[178]. In

---

175 See: C.R. Fox and A.N. Tversky, "Ambiguity Aversion and Comparative Ignorance", *Quarterly Journal of Economics*, Vol. 110, 1995, pp. 585-603.

176 Bruno Frey, *Happiness: A Revolution in Economics*, Cambridge, MA: The M.I.T. Press, 2008, p. 18.

177 Robert Axelrod, *The Evolution of Cooperation*, New York: Basic Books, 1984.

178 The prisoners' dilemma game refers to the following hypothetical situation: two criminals are arrested under the suspicion of having committed a crime together, and they care much more about their personal freedom than about the welfare of their accomplice. These prisoners are held separately, and the clever prosecutor makes attempts to induce each one to implicate the other. The 'dilemma' faced by the pris-

contrast to predictions of two-player game theory, Axelrod's empirical findings show that experimental subjects are frequently able to achieve cooperation rather than defection.

(vi) The 'Homo Economicus' model treats self-interest as if it were a natural law, thus ignoring the significance of 'cultural transmission'. Boyd and Richerson[179] have developed a model of cooperation based on "conformist transmission", which refers to the preferential selection of the behaviors individuals encounter most frequently. In other words, human beings are learning systems.

Given the above-mentioned defects of the classical concept of rationality, which leads to the axiomatization of the 'Economic Man', many social scientists have adopted a broader definition of 'rationality', according to which rationality implies only that individuals have well-ordered preference systems, each individual's preference system is essentially independent of the other economic variables, and every individual acts in order to maximize his utility index (the actors' goals can be interpreted to include a broad range of things, e.g. self-interest, altruism or any other quality). If one completely rejects the previous rationality principle, then this means that human behavior must be characterized only in some of the following ways: as strictly or primarily random, as instinctive, as strictly traditional, or as inherently inconsistent. However, this modified ra-

---

oners here is that, whatever the other does, each is better off confessing than remaining silent. But "the significant result here is that when both prisoners act selfishly by confessing, they both end up with long prison terms. Only when they act collusively or altruistically will they end up with short prison terms"; see: Samuelson and Nordhaus, *Economics*, p. 210. In any iterative prisoners' dilemma game, there is a certain maximum payoff each player can obtain by cooperating. But some strategies aim at finding ways of getting a little more with an occasional defection ('exploitation'). Axelrod argues that "a common problem with these rules is that they used complex methods of making inferences about the other player [strategy] — and these inferences were wrong"; thus, Axelrod's conclusion is "don't be too clever"; see: Axelrod, *The Evolution of Cooperation*, p. 120ff. Furthermore, Axelrod's empirical findings lead to an additional conclusion: "don't be envious"; Ibid., pp. 110–113.

179 Robert Boyd and P.J. Richerson, "Cultural Transmission and the Evolution of Cooperative Behavior", *Human Ecology*, Vol. 10, 1982, pp. 325-351.

tional choice theory does not assert merely that social behavior can be seen in terms of actors pursuing goals in general, but it makes assumptions about the *efficient* pursuit of *consistent* goals. Therefore, this modified rational choice theory is only a partially successful attempt to operationalize the old, defunct version of rational choice theory, which underpins classical microeconomics.

We can free economics from the defects of rational choice theory by taking the following two measures: (i) by asserting that rationality means only that social behavior can be seen in terms of actors pursuing goals; and (ii) by letting the actors' behaviors, as empirical data, speak to us about the actors' mentalities and goals, i.e., by understanding what the actors' actions, as empirical data, reveal to us about the actors' value system and strategy, instead of trying to explain social behavior through ideally-typical approximations of the actor's (rational or non-rational) essence.

Beyond rational choice theory

In chapter 1, I argued that action is an energy that aims at changing a given situation and that every conscious action is characterized by the dialectic of kairicity. In other words, in chapter 1, I argued that action, when it is an autonomous activity, and not a consequence of coercion or necessity, takes place according to a set of expediencies that has been freely accepted by the actor's consciousness. Moreover, this set of expediencies, which is based on the intentionality of consciousness, is connected with the intentionality of action.

Which is the cause of action, i.e., the link between the consciousness of action and the object of action? The answer to the previous question is values. As Louis Lavelle[180] has put it, a price is a fact whereas a value is a judgment (an act of the conscious mind). Moreover, according to R. Polin[181], by the term value, we should understand the "centre of interest" toward which consciousness is

---

180 Louis Lavelle, *Traité des Valeurs: Théorie Générale de la Valeur*, Paris: PUF, 1951; see also: J.J. Kockelmans (ed.), *Contemporary European Ethics*, New York: Anchor Books, 1972.

181 See: Kockelmans (ed.), *Contemporary European Ethics*.

directed whenever it is engaged in a practical activity. Hence, value transcends action and simultaneously it is embedded in action, in the sense that value is the structure of action and action confirms the existence of value. Furthermore, a value is the justification of a corresponding price.

The philosophies of value can be divided into two general categories: the first category consists of the philosophies of value that hold that the 'Good' exists independent of consciousness, and the second category consists of the philosophies that are based on hedonism, according to which pleasure is the only intrinsic good. René Le Senne[182] (1882–1954) has summarized various objectivist theories of value by arguing that the relation between consciousness and value is similar to the relation that, according to objectivist epistemology, connects consciousness with truth. According to Le Senne, values are not creations of consciousness, because the fact that consciousness searches for values implies that consciousness is unable to provide its own self with values. Similarly, Gabriel Marcel[183] has argued that each value is a particular mode of being, which enriches the basic modes of being that are studied in ontology.

In contrast to the objectivist theories of value, the subjectivist theories of value stress the right of each consciousness to formulate and defend its values according to its freedom. Sartre[184] argues that one's personal freedom is the unique foundation of values and that no one is obliged to accept any particular value. For Sartre, the human being is free because it is not a self (an "in-itself") but a presence-to-self (the transcendence or "nihilation" of one's self). This Sartrean argument implies that we are "other" to our selves and that, irrespective of what we are or what others ascribe to us, we are "in the manner of not being it", in the sense that we are able to assume a

---

182 See: R.W. Sellars, "The Spiritualism of Lavelle and Le Senne", *Philosophy and Phenomenological Research*, Vol. 11, 1951, pp. 386-393; René Le Senne, *Le Mensenge et le Caractère*, Paris: F. Alcan, 1930.

183 Gabriel Marcel, *Man Against Mass Society*, trans. G.S. Fraser, St Augustine's Press, 2007.

184 J.-P. Sartre, *Being and Nothingness*, trans. H.E. Barnes, New York: Washington Square Press, 1992 (originally published in French in 1943).

perspective in its regard. Hence, according to Sartre, we are responsible for our "world", we create our "world", as our existential horizon and, thus, our life-orienting fundamental "choice" is the source
of our value system. Moreover, before Sartre, Eudoxus of Cnidus (a
Greek astronomer, mathematician, scholar and student of Plato),
Aristippus of Cyrene (a Greek philosopher, student of Socrates and
founder of the hedonistic philosophical school), Epicurus (a Greek
philosopher and the founder of the school of philosophy called Epi-
cureanism) and Blaise Pascal (a French philosopher and probability
theorist) had already put forward various arguments for the subjectivity of values and for the subjective origin of values.

In the light of kairology and particularly in the light of the dialectic of kairicity, which I have defended in Chapter 1, the objectivist philosophy of value and the subjectivist philosophy of value can
be considered as the two components of a more general philosophy
of value that I call the kairological philosophy of value. According
to the kairological philosophy of value, consciousness is the source
of values, consciousness is experienced by itself as the ultimate
(i.e., the supreme) value and the model of all the other values, but,
once created by consciousness, values constitute a separate mental
world. Furthermore, within the framework of a dynamic process of
objectivation, values are objectivated in the fields of language, science, art, action and history.

Even though most values, as creations of consciousness, are subjective, they must be objectivated, because it is due to and through
their objectivation that consciousness can view them from some
distance and, hence, experience them more fully. According to
Lavelle, every value is the object of a desire and of a judgment, and,
therefore, the objectivation of values creates the necessary conditions under which expressions of desire and judgment are possible.
In other words, consciousness takes some distance from the values
that it creates in order to experience its attraction to them, and values have a tendency to return to consciousness. Through the previous dialectical game, consciousness confirms its dynamic imposition on values, since it is the creator and the consumer of values.
Additionally, in the previous dialectical game, consciousness acts

kairically, because it creates a mental world where consciousness moves toward values and values move toward consciousness. Thus, values are determined by the kairicity of consciousness.

As a result of the existence of values, the human being develops consciousness of existence, since, through values and due to values, the human being is aware that — as opposed to every other biological being — it is not necessarily determined by the 'physical objectivity', but it can control and change the physical conditions of its existence, instead of being pathetically controlled by them.

The existence of the human being takes place in the physical realm through natural functions of the body and the mind[185]. But, since the human being is able to decisively intervene in the fields of its natural energies and impulses, the defining characteristic of the human being is not nature itself, but it is an 'existential otherness' toward the common nature of the human beings, i.e., an existential otherness makes the human subject a unique existence. This is the essence of personhood.

Personhood is an empirical reality that is characterized by reference[186], and it is impossible without a form of conscious communication. Personhood refers to a personal existential will and a personal existential energy that aim at preserving the continuity of existence and at improving the existential conditions of consciousness, and they operate as an impulse to participate in the world (since con-

---

185 John Searle has made the following observations: "Consciousness, in short, is a biological feature of human and certain animal brains. It is caused by neurobiological processes and is as much a part of the natural biological order as any other biological features such as photosynthesis, digestion, or mitosis. This principle is the first stage in understanding the place of consciousness within our worldview...Conscious mental states and processes have a special feature not possessed by other natural phenomena, namely, subjectivity. It is this feature of consciousness that makes its study so recalcitrant to the conventional methods of biological and psychological research"; Searle, *The Rediscovery of the Mind*, pp. 90, 93.

186 John Searle has mentioned that "conscious states always have a content. One can never just be conscious, rather when one is conscious, there must be an answer to the question, 'What is one conscious of?'"; Ibid., p. 84. Additionally, see: John Campbell, *Reference and Consciousness*, Oxford: Clarendon Press, 2002.

---

sciousness assimilates the world) and as pure self-knowledge. Personhood is expressed through communication among conscious beings.

Due to values, action is not merely a quantitative issue but it is also a qualitative one. In other words, values transform quantitative data into qualitative ones, and, therefore, values are the cause due to which human action can overthrow an established order of things and give rise to a new order of things. Human action is necessarily dependent on values, in the sense that values are the necessary underpinnings of human creativity.

In the light of the arguments that I have put forward up to this point, rational choice theory has a fundamental ontological defect: it treats human beings as if they were like units of a social/ economic system. Therefore, in the context of rational choice theory, the 'system' becomes a mechanism that obeys its own terms and logic, it leads to the autonomy of economics from the real human needs and expediencies, and, finally, the 'system' is imagined to be an impersonal and ruthless mechanism that is responsible for the necessities that frustrate human beings. If we restrict ourselves to the rationality postulate without making any additional assumptions, then we find ourselves on the path to empirically insignificant economic theories. Furthermore, the emphasis that rational choice theory places on the assumption that each actor duplicates the activities of other actors is the ontological cause of the intellectual and moral poverty that characterizes classical and neoclassical political economy. Within the framework of rational choice theory, the 'system' operates as an autonomous and absolute authority, since it imposes its own will by defining the terms of economic development and it subjugates all political and social procedures to its internal 'logic'. Before anything else, the 'system' establishes the rules of 'economic correctness', i.e., it determines the conditions under which the survival of the economic actors is possible, and the morality of the 'system' is nothing else apart from its internal logic.

On the other hand, kairology — namely, the methodical study of the kairicity of consciousness — shows that economic reality (like reality in general) is characterized by plasticity, and it is submissive to the intentionality of human consciousness. Therefore, the interpretation of economic reality can be achieved through the experience of the relation between the reality of consciousness and the reality of the world. Kairological economics is concerned with the study of the relationship between the economic world as a tank of opportunities and the economic actor's consciousness as a tank of intentions. From the viewpoint of kairological economics, the keystone of economic analysis is the economic actors' ability to reconstruct and utilize economic reality according to the four-fold dialectic of kairicity.

CHAPTER 10. EFFICIENT-MARKET HYPOTHESIS, BEHAVIORAL FINANCE AND KAIROLOGICAL FINANCE

The Efficient-Market Hypothesis

The efficient-market hypothesis (EMH) was developed by Eugene Fama, professor of finance at the University of Chicago Booth School of Business, in the 1960s. According to Fama[187], an efficient securities market is one where security prices always fully reflect all available information. This means that 'market knows best' and 'no investor can beat the market'. The EMH is based on the following three assumptions:

(a) Investors are assumed to be rational actors and thus value securities rationally. Rational investors tend to value each security according to its fundamental value, i.e., mainly according to the Net Present Value (NPV) of its future cash flows discounted by a factor r that is a composite of the risk-free rate and the risk premium.

(b) Even though some investors do not act rationally, their trading is random and their trades cancel each other out without affecting prices.

---

187 Eugene Fama, "Efficient Capital Markets: A Review of Theory and Empirical Work", *Journal of Finance*, Vol. 25, 1970, pp. 383-417.

(c) The influences of irrational investors on prices are eliminated by rational arbitrageurs.

The efficient-market view implies that security prices incorporate all available information as soon as it becomes available and that prices adjust to new levels according to the new NPV of the securities' future cash flows. However, Fama distinguishes three different forms of the EMH:

(a) The weak form of the EMH: No investor can earn excess ('abnormal') returns by trading securities based solely on historical price or return information. In other words, future prices cannot be predicted by analyzing prices from the past.

(b) The semi-strong form of the EMH: No investor can earn excess ('abnormal') returns by trading securities based on publicly available information, because the prices of securities adjust to publicly available new information very rapidly and in an unbiased fashion. Excess ('abnormal') returns can be earned only if one uses inside information (i.e., information that is not publicly available).

(c) The strong form of the EMH: No investor can earn excess ('abnormal') returns by trading securities based on any information whether publicly available or not (i.e., every possible inside information becomes publicly available very rapidly, and, therefore, it is reflected into prices as it becomes available).

Even when investors do not trade rationally (i.e., they over-react or under-react to information), their trades are assumed to cancel each other out (under-reaction will be as frequent as over-reaction to information), and, therefore, the market overall remains efficient. Additionally, Fama argues, any lag in the response of prices to an event is short-term, and, therefore, in the long-run, the EMH is still valid.

In general, the EMH can be mathematically expressed as a Martingale process. A martingale process is a stochastic process in which the conditional expectation of the next value, given the current and preceding values, is the current value — symbolically:

$$E[X_{t+1}, \Omega t] = x_t$$

where x_t is a martingale with respect to the sequence of information sets (Ωt) if the expectation of x_{t+1} (in fact, x_{t+j} where $j = 1,2,...$)

conditional on all currently available information (Ω_t) equals the current value. In other words, x_t is the optimal predictor of all future values of x. A stochastic process y_t is a fair game with respect to the sequence of information sets (Ω_t) if the conditional expectation of y_{t+1} is zero — symbolically:

$E[y_{t+1}, \Omega_t] = 0$.

Thus, a Martingale difference sequence $y_{t+1} = x_{t+1} \mathbin{\text{---}} x_t$ is a fair game.

Busse and Green[188] have supported the EMH by studying the extent to which and the manner in which the Morning Call and Midway Call segments on CNBC TV affect prices and trading: "The segments report analysts' views about individual stocks and are broadcast when the market is open"; "prices respond to reports within seconds of initial mention with positive reports fully incorporated within one minute"; "trading intensity doubles in the first minute, with a significant increase in buyer- (seller-) initiated trades after positive (negative) reports".

On the other hand, the theory of technical analysis counters the EMH. In contrast to the EMH, technical analysts test historical data, attempting to establish specific rules for securities traders. The basic idea of technical analysis is that prices move in trends that are determined by the altering attitudes of investors toward various economic, political and psychological events. The main assumptions of technical analysis are the following:

(a) Market action discounts everything: prices are determined by the forces of supply and demand.

(b) Prices move in trends: after a trend has been established, the future price movement will most probably follow the same direction until something occurs to change its direction. A price trend does not reverse itself, but only external influences can reverse the established trend.

(c) History tends to repeat itself, since people tend to repeat themselves. The repetitive nature of price movements is attributed

188 J.A. Busse and T.C. Green, "Market Efficiency in Real Time", *Journal of Financial Economics*, Vol. 65, 2002, pp. 425-437.

to psychological factors. Thus, technical analysts use chart patterns to analyze market movements and explain trends.

Brown and Jennings[189] argue that "technical analysis, or the use of past prices to infer private information, has value in a model in which prices are not fully revealing and traders have rational conjectures about the relation between prices and signals". In particular, Brown and Jennings, using "a two period dynamic model of equilibrium", demonstrate that "rational investors use historical prices in forming their demands" and illustrate "the sensitivity of the value of technical analysis to changes in the values of the exogenous parameters". Additionally, Neftci[190] has shown that technical-analysis trading rules can be formalized as nonlinear predictors.

The debate over the empirical relevance of the EMH and the theory of technical analysis becomes more complicated when we study financial crises. For instance, the U.S. stock-market crash of October 1987 inspired several studies. On the one hand, Black[191], Fama[192] and Roll[193] seek to explain the crash in terms of shifts in fundamental factors, e.g. downward revisions in expectations about global economic activity, higher equilibrium required returns, etc. On the other hand, Seyhun[194], after analyzing the behavior of corporate insiders, concludes that investor overreaction was an important part

189 D.P. Brown and R.H. Jennings, "On Technical Analysis", *The Review of Financial Studies*, Vol. 2, 1989, pp. 527-551.

190 S.N. Neftci, "Naïve Trading Rules in Financial Markets and Wiener-Kolmogorov Prediction Theory: A Study of 'Technical Analysis'", *Journal of Business*, Vol. 64, 1991, pp. 549-571.

191 Fischer Black, "An Equilibrium Model of the Crash", *NBER Macroeconomics Annual 1988*, Vol. 3, pp. 269-276, National Bureau of Economic Research, Inc.

192 Eugene Fama, "Perspectives on October 1987, Or What Did We Learn from the Crash?", in R.W. Kamphuis, Jr, R.C. Kormendi and J.W. Henry Watson (eds), *Black Monday and the Future of the Financial Markets*, Homewood, Ill.: Irwin, 1989, pp. 71-82.

193 Richard Roll, "The International Crash of October 1987", *Financial Analysis Journal*, Vol. 44, 1988, pp. 19-35.

194 H.N. Seyhun, "Overreaction of Fundamentals: Some Lessons from Insiders' Response to the Market Crash of 1987", *Journal of Finance*, Vol. 45, 1990, pp. 1363-1388.

of the crash. Moreover, Van Norden and Schaller[195], using regime-switching regressions, conclude that the degree of prior market overvaluations explains subsequent U.S. stock-market crashes for the period 1926–1989. In addition, there is a large literature on international currency crises. One strand of this literature seeks to develop early warning signals of exchange-rate crises; for instance, Kaminsky, Lizondo and Reinhardt[196] reviewed the results of 25 selected studies on currency crises and identified 103 crisis indicators. A second strand of the literature on international currency crises examines the issue of 'currency contagion'; for instance, Sachs, Tornell and Velasco[197] show that countries with weak fundamentals are more susceptible to currency contagion.

Behavioral finance

According to the EMH, because actors are rational and there are no frictions, a security's price equals its 'fundamental value'. In other words, under the EMH, 'prices are right', in the sense that they are set by actors who understand Bayes's theorem[198] and have sensible preferences. Hence, in an efficient market, 'there is no free meal', in the sense that no investment can yield excess risk-adjusted average returns, i.e., average returns greater than are warranted for its risk. In contrast to the EMH, behavioral finance argues that some features of asset prices are most plausibly interpreted as deviations from fundamental value and that these deviations are consequences

195 Simon van Norden and Huntley Schaller, "Speculative Behaviour, Regime-Switching and Stock Market Crashes", Bank of Canada Working Paper 96-13, October 1996.

196 Graciela Kaminsky, Saúl Lizondo and Carmen Reinhardt, "Leading Indicators of Currency Crises", International Monetary Fund, Western Hemisphere Department, Working Paper No. WP/97/79, July 1997.

197 Jeffrey Sachs, Aaron Tornell and Andreas Velasco, "The Mexican Peso Crisis: Sudden Death or Death Foretold?", *Journal of International Economics*, Vol. 41, 1996, pp. 351-366. Also, see: Marcel Fratzscher, "On Currency Crises and Contagion", European Central Bank, Working Paper Series 139, April 2002.

198 Put simply, Beyes's theorem asserts that the probability of an event A given an event B depends not only on the relation between events A and B but also on the marginal probability of occurrence of each event.

of the presence of traders who are not fully rational. According to behavioral finance, the following psychological factors play important role in the formation of financial behavior and particularly in the formation of expectations[199]:

(a) Overconfidence: This attitude appears in two guises. First, the confidence intervals people assign to their quantitative estimations are far too narrow; according to Alpert and Raiffa[200], many persons' 98% confidence intervals include the true quantity only about 60% of the time. Second, according to Fischhoff, Slovic and Lichtenstein[201], "people [are] wrong too often when they are certain that they are right".

(b) Optimism bias: it includes over-estimating the likelihood of positive events and under-estimating the likelihood of negative events. Optimism bias can result in cost overruns, benefit shortfalls and delays in the implementation of projects. Armor and Taylor[202] have reviewed a number of studies that have found optimism bias in different kinds of judgment: second-year MBA students overestimated the number of job offers they would receive and their starting salary; students overestimated the scores they would achieve on exams; newlyweds expected their marriage to last a lifetime, even though they were aware of the divorce statistics; professional financial analysts overestimated corporate earnings; most smokers believed that they were less at risk

---

199 For more details, see: Nicholas Barberis, Andrei Shleifer and Robert Vishny, "A Model of Investor Sentiment", *Journal of Financial Economics*, Vol. 49, 1998, pp. 307-345; Daniel Kahneman and Amos Tversky (eds), *Choices, Values and Frames*, Cambridge: Cambridge University Press, 2000; Daniel Kahneman, Paul Slovic and Amos Tversky (eds), *Judgment Under Uncertainty: Heuristics and Biases*, Cambridge: Cambridge University Press, 1982.

200 Marc Alpert and Howard Raiffa, "A Progress Report on the Training of Probability Assessors", in D. Kahneman, P. Slovic and A. Tversky (eds), *Judgment Under Uncertainty*, pp. 294-305.

201 Baruch Fischhoff, Paul Slovic and Sarah Lichtenstein, "Knowing with Certainty: The Appropriateness of Extreme Confidence", *Journal of Experimental Psychology*, Vol. 3, 1977, pp. 552-564.

202 D.A. Armor and S.E. Taylor (eds), "When Predictions Fail: The Dilemma of Unrealistic Optimism", in T. Gilovich, D. Griffin and D. Kahneman (eds), *Heuristics and Biases: The Psychology of Intuitive Judgment*, Cambridge: Cambridge University Press, 2002, pp. 334-347.

---

of developing smoking-related diseases than other members of the population of smokers.

(c) Representativeness Heuristic: Tversky and Kahneman have explained this kind of behavior as follows:

> Many of the probabilistic questions with which people are concerned belong to one of the following types: What is the probability that object A belongs to class B? What is the probability that event A originates from process B? What is the probability that process B will generate event A? In answering such questions, people typically rely on the representativeness heuristic, in which probabilities are evaluated by the degree to which A is representative of B, that is, by the degree to which A resembles B...This approach to the judgment of probability leads to serious errors, because similarity, or representativeness, is not influenced by several factors that should affect judgments of probability...Insensitivity to prior probability of outcomes. One of the factors that have no effect on representativeness but should have a major effect on probability is the prior probability, or base-rate frequency, of the outcomes...Insensitivity to sample size...Misconceptions of chance...Insensitivity to predictability... The illusion of validity...Misconceptions of regression.[203]

(d) Conservatism: According to Edwards[204], people are slow to change their beliefs in the face of new evidence. Thus, investors subject to conservatism "might disregard the full information content of an earnings announcement", perhaps because "this number contains a large temporary component" and "they still cling at least partially to their prior estimates of earnings"[205].

(e) Belief perseverance: According to Lord, Ross and Lepper[206], there is much evidence that, once people have formed an opinion, they cling to it too tightly and for too long.

---

203 Amos Tversky and Daniel Kahneman, "Judgment under Uncertainty: Heuristics and Biases", *Science*, New Series, Vol. 185, 1974, pp. 1124-1127.

204 Ward Edwards, "Conservatism in Human Information Processing", in B. Kleinmutz (ed.), *Formal Representation of Human Judgment*, New York: John Wiley and Sons, 1968.

205 Andrei Shleifer, *Inefficient Markets: An Introduction to Behavioural Finance*, Oxford: Oxford University Press, 2000, p. 128.

206 Charles Lord, Lee Ross and Mark Lepper, "Biased Assimilation and Attitude Polarization: The Effect of Theories on Subsequently Considered Evidence", *Journal of Personality and Social Psychology*, Vol. 37, 1979, pp. 2098-2109.

(f) Adjustment and anchoring: Tversky and Kahneman have explained this kind of behavior as follows:

> In many situations, people make estimates by starting from an initial value that is adjusted to yield the final answer. The initial value, or starting point, may be suggested by the formulation of the problem, or it may be the result of a partial computation. In either case, adjustments are typically insufficient. That is, different starting points yield different estimates, which are biased toward the initial values. We call this phenomenon anchoring.[207]

(g) Availability biases: Tversky and Kahneman have explained this kind of behavior as follows:

> There are situations in which people assess the frequency of a class or the probability of an event by the ease with which instances or occurrences can be brought to mind. For example, one may assess the risk of heart attack among middle-aged people by recalling such occurrences among one's acquaintances. Similarly, one may evaluate the probability that a given business venture will fail by imagining various difficulties it could encounter. This judgmental heuristic is called availability. Availability is a useful clue for assessing frequency or probability... However, availability is affected by factors other than frequency and probability. Consequently, the reliance on availability leads to predictable biases...Biases due to the effectiveness of a search set...Biases due to retrievability of instances...Biases of imaginability...Illusory correlation.[208]

Kairological finance

From the above survey of the literature on the EMH and on behavioral finance, it follows that neither the EMH nor behavioral finance gives sufficient guarantees that it can cover the entire field of finance: the EMH expresses only rational processes and the ability of consciousness to control itself; behavioral finance stresses irrational processes and the inner vibrations of the human subject. Beyond all these partial principles, lies the art of combining all the aspects of financial life together, and this combination is not only the goal but it is also the presupposition of kairic action, through which the intentionality of consciousness is manifested in the field of finance. This is the essence of what I call 'kairological finance'. In fact, in or-

---

207 Tversky and Kahneman, "Judgment under Uncertainty", p. 1128.
208 Ibid., pp. 1127–1128.

der to act kairically and hence to improve its existential conditions, consciousness gathers and uses all its forces — both rational and non-rational ones, i.e., logic, feelings, instincts and intuition.

CHAPTER 11. KAIROLOGICAL GROWTH THEORY

From the standpoint of kairology, the kairicity of human con-sciousness is the most important factor of production, because it extends the ability of the conventional factors of production — i.e., labor, capital and land — to produce wealth. Moreover, the kairic action of consciousness increases the quantity of final goods, and these goods, in turn, underpin the continuation of the kairic action of consciousness.

The growth model that was formulated by the classical econo-mists is based on the principle of the scarcity of resources, and it has the tendency to imprison economic thought in a 'given' economic reality: "goods are scarce because there are not enough resources to produce all the goods that people want to consume. All of econom-ics flows from this central fact"[209]. However, kairology shows that reality is not a 'given', but, ultimately, it is created by the intention-ality of human consciousness. Thus, we need a new growth theory — one that will comply with kairology.

The kairological growth theory that I present in this section shows the manner in which kairicity reduces scarcity to satisfy human needs and desires. First, I shall review the main features of

---

209 Samuelson and Nordhaus, *Economics*, p. 8.

the classical growth model. The conception of labor that dominates classical economics is intimately related to the notion of physical labor. Physical labor extracts economic goods from resources and requires energy, i.e., food. An economy that is based only on physical labor operates according to the following empirical principle: the quantity of food produced in a working day is equal to the quantity of food the labor force consumes to be able to work along the day. According to this principle, the notion of 'exploitation' is equivalent to the notion of 'profit': for instance, assume that a worker needs 10 units of food to carry out 1 day of work (so that he can reconstitute his working strength) and that he produces 10 units of food in a working day; then, to get a profit, one must pay this worker with a salary less than 10 units of food.

Moreover, for classical economists, a tool is merely a quantity of labor integrated in an object[210]. Marx calls it "dead labor". "Capital is dead labor", Marx writes, "that, vampire-like, only lives by sucking living labor, and lives the more, the more labor it sucks"[211]. Tools always require labor to be constructed. For example, assume that a worker needs 10 working days to construct a tool. According to the labor theory of value[212], any tool can provide an output of goods equal to the dead labor that is integrated into it. Thus, in our example, the given tool can only produce an output of goods equivalent to 10 working days. Moreover, if, as we assumed earlier, a working

210 In the 15th chapter of the first volume of K. Marx's book *The Capital*, Marx studies machinery and large-scale industry, and, after stating that "a tool [is] a simple machine and a machine a complex tool", he argues that only labor power, which is bought by capitalists, can create new value and that the machine accumulates value from the labor, which went into producing it, and it merely transfers its value into the product it is producing.

211 Karl Marx, *The Capital*, New York: International Publishers, 1987, Vol. 1, p. 224 (originally published in 1867).

212 "An economy in which prices are determined by the amount of labor that goes into the production of each commodity is governed by the labor theory of value. In an economy such as Smith described, average labor cost would determine price no matter how many goods there were"; see: Samuelson and Nordhaus, *Economics*, p. 548.

day produces 10 units of food, then the given tool will produce 100 units of food.

According to the classical growth model, which I have just reviewed, growth is explained as follows: Growth results in first by adding more labor to increase output. But, since resources are limited, labor suffers diminishing returns. As population grows, output decreases, despite the fact that the input of labor increases[213]. Capital (tools and machines) is mainly conceived as dead labor, and, it cannot be exploited like active labor. According to Marx's law of decreasing profits, capitalists compete for introducing new machinery in order to gain as much profit as possible, and, therefore, because of excessive accumulation of capital, profit is gradually reduced[214]. As a conclusion, according to the classical growth model, growth is determined by the production possibility frontier[215] (efficiency implies that the economy is on its production-possibility frontier). Within this framework of analysis, growth necessarily stops when the marginal revenue product[216] equals marginal factor cost[217].

---

213 "The classical models of Smith and Malthus describe economic development in terms of fixed land and growing population. In the absence of technological change, increasing population ultimately exhausts the supply of free land. The resulting increase in population density triggers the law of diminishing returns. With less and less land to work, each new worker adds less and less extra product; as a result, competitive wages fall while land rents go up"; see: Ibid., p. 563.

214 "In the beginning, there is a gradual increase of the amount of capital per worker, or 'capital deepening'. In the absence of technological change and innovation, an increase in capital per worker would not be matched by a proportional increase in output per worker because of diminishing returns. Hence, capital deepening would lower the rate of return on capital (equal to the real interest rate under risk-free competition)"; see: Ibid., p. 563.

215 "The production-possibility frontier (or PPF) shows the maximum amounts of production that can be obtained by an economy, given the technological knowledge and quantity of inputs available. The PPF represents the menu of choices available to society"; see: Ibid., p. 22.

216 Marginal revenue product is the additional revenue generated by the employment or use of an extra variable input.

217 Marginal factor cost is the additional cost incurred by employing or using an additional factor unit.

However, the previous classical model of economic growth, by remaining intellectually anchored in the scarcity of resources, cannot really explain economic growth. Various studies that follow the techniques of growth accounting have broken down the growth of GNP in the private business sector into its contributing factors and they have shown that the contribution of education and technological change to output growth is bigger than the contribution of capital. For instance, Robert Solow[218] has found that, in the United States, during the period 1909–1949, about one-eighth of the increment in labor productivity could be attributed to increased capital per man hour, and the remaining seven-eighths to a factor that is called "Solow residual" and consists of technological progress and other cultural factors that improve efficiency. Edward F. Denison[219] has studied the contribution of different elements to growth in real GNP in the United States during the period 1929–1982, and he has shown that advances in knowledge, education and other cultural-institutional factors play the most important role in economic growth, as displayed in the following table.

Before the research works of Solow and Denison, Henri Fayol (1841–1925), a French mining engineer and director of mines who developed a theory of business administration, had emphasized that cultural issues and technical improvements are key factors for growth. In particular, Fayol has argued that managers must be able to give orders and simultaneously they must be kind and fair to their subordinates. Moreover, according to Fayol's principles of management, people and materials should be in the right place at the right time. In a similar spirit, Frederick Winslow Taylor (1856–1915), an American mechanical engineer who sought to improve industrial efficiency and is regarded as the father of scientific management, has argued that even the most basic tasks could be planned in a way that would increase productivity.

---

218 R.M. Solow, "Technical Change and the Aggregate Production Function", *Review of Economics and Statistics*, Vol. 39, 1957, pp. 312-320.
219 E.F. Denison, *Trends in American Economic Growth, 1929–1982*, Washington, DC: Brookings, 1985; E.F. Denison, *Multifactor Productivity Measures*, 1988 and 1989, U.S. Department of Labor, March 1991.

Relative contributions to U.S. growth, 1929–1982:		
	Percent contribution to total growth of 2.9% per year on average	*Percent contribution to per-person growth of 1.5% per year on average*
Source		
Labor input except education	32	–12
Education per worker	14	27
Capital	19	20
Advances in knowledge	20	38
Improved resource allocation	8	16
Economies of scale	9	18
Land	0	–3
Changes in legal and human environment	–1	–3

In general, we realize that kairicity increases the quantity of goods produced by labor and capital because it integrates ideas in labor and capital. For instance, in the 19th century, application of the Frank B. Gilbreth system of motion analysis in bricklaying reduced the motions per brick from 18 to 5 and increased the number of bricks laid per hour from 125 to 350; thus, this system has helped U.S. labor compete with other countries which have lower pay scales. This is an example that shows that the integration of ideas in labor is the sole reason for the increase in production. Moreover, the integration of ideas in capital (tools and machines) multiplies production. For instance, Frederick W. Taylor, in his study of the "science of shovelling", found that the optimal weight that a worker should lift in a shovel was 21 pounds, and, therefore, the shovel should be sized so that it would hold 21 pounds of the substance being shovelled; the firm provided the workers with optimal shovels, and the results were a three to four fold increase in productivity and pay increases for the workers.

Classical political economy is focused on the principle that resources are limited and leads to the conclusion that we should expect a 'limit to growth'. In 1972, the Club of Rome published a book entitled *The Limits to Growth*[220] (written by Donella H. Meadows, Dennis L. Meadows, J. Randers and W.W. Behrens III), according to which, within a time span of less than 100 years with no major change in the physical, economic, or social relations that have traditionally governed world development, society will run out of the non-renewable resources on which the industrial economy depends. However, the kairic action of consciousness can rearrange the resources and also create an additional resource base.

Even if resources are limited, kairicity enables us to get more from the existing resources by transforming-rearranging them. Energy transitions from wood to coal and from coal to oil provide important examples of the contribution of the kairic action of consciousness to economic growth. Paul M. Romer, an American economist and entrepreneur, associated with the New York University Stern School of Business and with Stanford University, has put forward the following argument:

> Economic growth occurs whenever people take resources and rearrange them in ways that are more valuable. A useful metaphor for production in an economy comes from the kitchen. To create valuable final products, we mix inexpensive ingredients together according to a recipe. The cooking one can do is limited by the supply of ingredients, and most cooking in the economy produces undesirable side effects. If economic growth could be achieved only by doing more and more of the same kind of cooking, we would eventually run out of raw materials and suffer from unacceptable levels of pollution and nuisance. History teaches us, however, that economic growth springs from better recipes, not just from more cooking. New recipes generally produce fewer unpleasant side effects and generate more economic value per unit of raw material...Every generation has perceived the limits to growth that finite resources and undesirable side effects would pose if no new recipes or ideas were discovered. And every generation has underestimated the potential for finding new recipes and ideas. We consistently fail to grasp how

---

220 D.H. Meadows et al., *The Limits to Growth*, New York: University Books, 1972.

many ideas remain to be discovered. Possibilities do not add up. They multiply.[221]

In fact, the most important source of change and progress is kairicity. The kairic action of consciousness can create an additional resource base, since science and technology enable us to create a practically unlimited artificial resource base. Additionally, Alvin Toffler has made the following observations:

> As service and information sectors grow in the advanced economies, as manufacturing itself is computerized, the nature of wealth necessarily changes. While investors in backward sectors of industry still regard the traditional 'hard assets' — plant, equipment, and inventories — as critical, investors in the fastest growing, most advanced sectors rely on radically different factors to back their investments. No one buys a share of Apple Computer or IBM stock because of the firm's material assets. What counts are not the company's buildings or machines but the contacts and power of its marketing and sales force, the organizational capacity of its management, and the ideas crackling inside the heads of its employees...The shift to this new form of capital explodes the assumptions that underpin both Marxist ideology and classical economics.[222]

Kairological growth theory combines the notion of sustainable development[223] with the notion of unlimited growth. 'Sustainability' invites us to be aware of our environmental conditions and act as responsible beings in order to preserve life. According to Fivos Papadimitriou, "a rural landscape is sustainable under its contemporary land management and land-use regime if two conditions hold: (1) the landscape is physically viable for the present and the future, and (2) the population acting on and living from he natural resources of the landscape is socio-economically viable in the pres-

221 P.M. Romer, "Compound Rates of Growth"; in:
http://www.econlib.org/library/Enc/EconomicGrowth.html
Additionally, see: P.M. Romer, "Endogenous Technological Change", *Journal of Political Economy*, Vol. 98, 1990, pp. 71–102.

222 Alvin Toffler, *Powershift: Knowledge, Wealth and Violence at the Edge of the 21ˢᵗ Century*, New York: Bantam Books, 1991, p. 73.

223 United Nations, "Report of the World Commission on Environment and Development", General Assembly Resolution 42/187, December 11, 1987.

ent and the future"[224]. However, sustainability should not lead us to the assumption that there are any given 'limits to growth'. Because of man's kairic intervention in the reality of the world, there is not a single optimum point for environmental management and economic growth, but there are several, arguably infinitely many, such optimal points, since the creativity of the human mind is unlimited and a kairic consciousness continuously acts in order to restructure and utilize the reality of the world in the most favorable manner.

224 Fivos Papadimitriou, "Landscape Sustainability", in P. Mairota, J.B. Thornes and N. Geeson (eds), *Atlas of Mediterranean Environments in Europe: The Desertification Context*, West Sussex: John Wiley & Sons, 1998, pp. 72-74.

Chapter 12. Kairicity, Distributive Justice And The Ethical Content Of Economics

When the consciousness of existence formulates judgments, it is called moral consciousness. In other words, moral consciousness is the consciousness of existence itself when it operates as a judge. Moral consciousness seems to be innate, because, even though it is *affected* by social structure, it is not *created* by social structure. Moral consciousness internalizes and reflects social values, and it may be forced to comply with social values, but it can always judge and criticize social values, conceive the idea of a more just society and even revolt. Hence, far from being a mere creation of society, moral consciousness transcends the established social structure.

With respect to its operation, moral consciousness is composed of sentimental elements (e.g. respect, pride, indignation and guilt), intellectual elements and volitional elements. The sentimental factor, the intellectual factor and the volitional factor of moral consciousness are inseparable from each other, but the sentimental factor is the strongest one, because it plays the predominant role in the formation of moral consciousness. For instance, an idea, i.e., an intellectual element of moral consciousness, may be ambiguous, and, therefore, moral consciousness may not be able to make decisions on the basis of the given idea, but, if it has a clear sentimental orientation, moral consciousness may be able to make a clear and accurate evaluation of the situation in which it has to act. More-over, the volitional factor may be weak, and, therefore, it may be unable to lead moral consciousness to a clear decision, but, if it has a clear sentimental orientation, moral consciousness may remain strong and lively and make clear decisions.

Jeremy Bentham's utilitarianism

Jeremy Bentham[225] (1748–1832), the English moral philosopher, jurist, social reformer, political economist and founding father of modern utilitarianism, exerted significant influence on classical po-litical economy. Bentham stressed the importance of the quantity of pleasure, and, in fact, his moral philosophy consists in a "felicific calculus", which has been explained and summarized by J.V. Orth as follows:

> Happiness could be gauged by a 'felicific calculus'. Four circum-stances determine the value of a pleasure in isolation: intensity, duration, certainty, and propinquity. Two other factors, in addi-tion, affect the value of a pleasure in a lifetime: fecundity (for ex-ample, the likelihood of being followed by more pleasures) and purity (for example, the likelihood of being followed by pain). And, since Bentham was concerned with the common good, he added a final factor: the extent of the pleasure or the number of persons affected by it.[226]

According to Bentham's arithmetic of pleasures, the quality of pleasures ultimately reduces to their quantity or at least to their intensity. Hence, the major defect of Bentham's moral philosophy is that it is unable to address qualitative issues. Furthermore, another important defect of Bentham's moral philosophy is his argument that the value of a pleasure depends on the number of the persons that are affected by it; the previous principle is problematic because of the following reasons: (i) even though Bentham argues that the

---

225 Jeremy Bentham, *An Introduction to the Principles of Morals and Legislation*, ed. J.H. Burns and H.L.A. Hart, London: Athlone Press, 1970 (originally published in 1789).

226 See: J.V. Orth, "Jeremy Bentham: The Common Law's Severest Critic", *American Bar Association Journal*, Vol. 68, 1982, p. 714.

same pleasure can be experienced by different subjects, the evaluation of each pleasure is a subjective question; (ii) even though one may accept that he has moral duties, he may define them in accordance with his individual interests, and, therefore, Bentham's moral philosophy may reduce to a justification of egoism; (iii) in the context of Bentham's moral philosophy, the protection of the general interest of society may lead to the suppression of the individual, since Bentham has not formulated any universal moral criterion capable of uniting different individuals into a harmonious whole.

John Stuart Mill's utilitarianism

John Stuart Mill[227] (1806–1873), the most influential English-speaking philosopher of the nineteenth century and a major representative of classical political economy, attempted to liberate utilitarianism from the antinomies and defects of Bentham's moral philosophy, and, therefore, he has argued that utility as a moral criterion is of a qualitative nature, and not of a quantitative one. According to J.S. Mill, if one overlooks the qualitative dimension of pleasure, then he arrives at a moral theory "worthy only of swine". Additionally, according to J.S. Mill, "it is better to be a human being dissatisfied than a pig satisfied". Thus, for Mill, the general interest of society must be respected and get priority because of its intrinsic value and not because it may coincide with people's individual interests. Moreover, Mill's golden rule of utilitarian morality is to do as you would be done by and to love your neighbor. Hence, Mill's utilitarian morality implies that only a pleasure that is intrinsically noble is worthy to be experienced by the human being. The foundation of Mill's utilitarian morality is the value of being human itself.

Even though J.S. Mill has managed to improve Bentham's utilitarian moral philosophy, Mill's moral philosophy is also problematic due to antinomies that are intrinsic to utilitarianism itself. Mill argues that there is an empirical criterion for the qualitative evalu-

---

227 See: Karl Britton, John Stuart Mill, Harmondsworth: Penguin, 1953; Roger Crisp, Mill on Utilitarianism, London: Routledge, 1997; Pedro Schwartz, *The New Political Economy of J.S. Mill*, London: Weidenfeld & Nicolson, 1972.

ation of pleasures and that this criterion is unerringly manifested in the conscious minds of the most scientifically cultivated and knowledgeable people. But even the conscious minds of the most scientifically cultivated and knowledgeable people are not infallible. Moreover, according to Mill, if no other factors (such as restrictions, coercion, etc.) interfere, consciousness is attracted, and it should be attracted, to the noblest pleasures, and, therefore, Mill makes a logically illegitimate inference from 'is' to 'ought', from 'is desired' to 'is worthy of desire', and G.E. Moore[228] has called it the "naturalistic fallacy". Finally, J.S. Mill has not answered the following question: since there is no criterion of morality that transcends pleasure, on what grounds can one view a specific pleasure as superior to all other pleasures? In general, utilitarianism overemphasizes the notion of interest, and, therefore, it overemphasizes the antithesis among individual interests and the need to harmonize individual interests, but, since utilitarianism lacks any criterion of morality that transcends pleasure, the attempt to build social harmony on the basis of utilitarianism is chimerical.

Adam Smith's theory of moral sentiments

Adam Smith (1723–1790), the founder of classical political economy, published *The Theory of Moral Sentiments* in 1759, and he is the main representative of the morality of sympathy.

According to Adam Smith, 'sympathy' is the intuitive perception of the normative character of human behavior. Smith relates sympathy to approval as follows:

> To approve of another man's opinions is to adopt those opinions, and to adopt them is to approve of them. If the same arguments which convince you convince me likewise, I necessarily approve of your conviction; and if they do not, I necessarily disapprove of it; neither can I possibly convince that I should do the one without the others. To approve or disapprove, therefore, of the opinions of others is acknowledged, by every body, to mean no more than to observe their agreement or disagreement with our

---

228 G.E. Moore, *Principia Ethica*, New York: Prometheus Books, 1988 (originally published in 1903).

own. But it is equally the case with regard to our approbation or disapprobation of the sentiments or passions of others.[229]

Similarly, he argues:

> To approve of the passions of another...as suitable to their objects, is the same thing as to observe that we entirely sympathize with them; and not to approve of them as such, is the same thing as to observe that we do not entirely sympathize with them. The man who resents the injuries that have been done to me, and observes that I resent them precisely as he does, necessarily approves of my resentment. The man whose sympathy keeps time to my grief, cannot but admit the reasonableness of my sorrow.[230]

Smith argues that sympathy, of which we must become worthy, must have the following characteristics: (i) it must be pure and unconditional (since, in the field of moral sentiments, ambiguity implies suspicious actions); (ii) it must be universal, i.e., experienced by everybody, or at least by the majority of the people. But the following question emerges: what should one do in case he does not know if others approve or disapprove of his actions? Smith answered the previous question as follows: he should act as an impartial spectator of his own actions, so that his own judgment can be used as a substitute for other persons' approval or disapproval of his actions.

Adam Smith's moral philosophy has the following defects: (i) Sympathy is not as universal as Smith wishes, because it is not a necessary conscious state, and it may vary from one consciousness to another. (ii) Sympathy can be influenced by non-rational factors, and, therefore, it cannot lead to the formulation of moral judgments that are immune to criticism. (iii) By arguing that the actor's own consciousness can be used as a substitute for the consciousness of a sympathizing spectator-judge whenever the first operates as an impartial spectator, Smith eliminates sympathy (resp. antipathy) in those fields in which sympathy (resp. antipathy) is presupposed (i.e., in the fields of moral deliberation and judgment); this is a logi-

---

229 Adam Smith, *The Theory of Moral Sentiments*, ed. D.D. Raphael and A.L. Macfie, Oxford: Oxford University Press, 1976 (originally published in 1759), p. 17.
230 Ibid., p. 16.

cal contradiction. In other words, the major logical contradiction of Smith's moral philosophy is the following: Smith argues that sympathy is a moral sentiment, but, in practice, he interprets sympathy as an expression of moral rationality.

Immanuel Kant's moral rationalism

Modern political economy being founded on rational choice theory, it necessary follows that a form of moral rationalism is implicitly or explicitly embedded in every theory of classical and neoclassical economics. In the history of modern philosophy, the most influential theory of moral rationalism was formed by Immanuel Kant[231].

Kant developed a new moral theory by shifting the debate about morality from actions to intentions. His most influential positions are found in *The Groundwork of the Metaphysics of Morals*, but he developed, enriched, and in some cases modified those views in later works such as *The Critique of Practical Reason, The Metaphysics of Morals, Anthropology from a Pragmatic Point of View* and *Religion within the Boundaries of Mere Reason*. Subscribing to J.-J. Rousseau's thesis that nothing is absolutely good in this world or out of it except a good intention, Kant added that a good intention is good not because its consequences are good but because it is intrinsically good. Hence, for Kant, an act is moral if its sole motive is pure respect for the moral law, assuming, of course, that it is combined with adequate action. Moreover, Kant emphasizes that the moral law is a categorical imperative, i.e., it commands unconditionally. According to Kant the ultimate criterion of morality is the following: always act so that you can will that everybody shall follow the determining principle of your action. For instance, no rational being can will that everybody should make lying promises, for, if everybody did, nobody would believe anybody and finally lying promises would prove to be self-defeating. No rational being can really will a contradiction,

---

231 See: Bruce Aune, *Kant's Theory of Morals*, Princeton, NJ: Princeton University Press, 1979; Paul Guyer (ed.), *Kant's Groundwork of the Metaphysics of Morals: Critical Essays*, Lantham, MD: Rowman and Littlefield, 1998.

and a lying promise is a contradiction. Similarly, no rational being can will to disregard the welfare of others, because, if everybody did the same, the given being itself might some day become the victim of inhuman behavior. Thus, Kant emphasizes that the rational will imposes upon itself universal laws.

Kant's moral theory has the following major defects: (i) Kant's thesis that nothing is intrinsically and absolutely good in this world or out of it except a good intention is wrong. A characteristic counter-example to Kant's previous assertion is 'knowledge'; knowledge is an epistemological value and not an intention, but it is intrinsically and absolutely good (knowledge is always morally superior to ignorance). (ii) Kant's thesis that the moral law is a categorical imperative leads to oversimplification. A characteristic counter-example to Kant's previous assertion is the following: if you know that someone asks you information about another person in order to harm it, then it may be neither psychologically easy nor rational to be sincere. The logical power and consistence of Kant's moral theory can be purchased at too high a cost — namely, the elimination of sensitivity and generally the elimination of the sentimental factor in moral life. But, by eliminating sensitivity and generally the sentimental factor in moral life, Kant's morality deprives the human being of powerful motives that contribute to the development of a fully integrated moral consciousness.

Finally, contra Kant and Kant's moral philosophy, Michel Anteby, a professor in the organizational behavior area at Harvard University, has pointed out that so-called "moral grey zones" exist in more or less every sector or enterprise, and they "emerge when official company rules are repeatedly broken with, at minimum, a supervisor's tacit or explicit approval". Anteby gives the following examples:

> Since their delivery routes and tasks are highly controlled, the choices postal carriers make about delivering mail are fairly constrained. However, a carrier who wishes to deliver mail to a given home earlier than the official schedule dictates is often encouraged to do so by his supervisor, albeit without any official endorsement of changes to the delivery route schedule. Carriers who participate in such activities and finish their routes before the workday officially ends often engage in 'hiding'…The

carriers operate in a gray zone...They are able to end their day earlier by modifying the schedule of delivery...Mail carriers are not alone in alerting us to the interplay between gray zones and occupational identities. The behaviors of construction crews, paramedics, and emergency medical technicians also showcase this interplay. Threatened with delays in the work schedule by property owners who insist that machinery and workers remain strictly in the right of way...members of the pipeline construction crew might arrange with the supervisors to offer property owners some simple labor in exchange for the latitude to get their job done quickly...Paramedics and emergency medical technicians (EMTs)...provide another illustration of occupational dynamics at play in gray zones...physicians often afford paramedics and EMTs considerable leeway to 'play doctor' or 'experiment' with certain drugs and dosages when they believe it critical to a patient's survival.[232]

Thus, moral grey zones rely on personal trust, at all levels, and of course this attitude is not appropriate in all contexts. However, this flexible approach to official rules increases competition within the workplace and the impetus of staff to prove themselves, bringing a greater desire for autonomy and challenge, and cultivates discretion and critical thought.

The need for a kairological morality

Pleasures express man's attraction to life; sentiments are ideas endowed with emotions; and reason expresses the power of consciousness to control itself. However, all the previous moral criteria can be combined into a kairological morality, which leads to kairic action and is a presupposition of kairic action. Kairological morality expresses the intentionality of consciousness, which, in turn, is expressed as an itinerary toward a better life and utilizes the sentimental factor, the intellectual factor and the volitional factor of moral consciousness in order to be confirmed.

---

232 Michel Anteby, *Moral Gray Zones*, Princeton: Princeton University Press, 2008, pp. 142–143.

Contemporary moral debates in the academic discipline of Economics

Economics is intimately related to moral questions. For instance, economists are concerned with questions of the following type: What sorts of inequalities are morally acceptable in a just society? How extensive can inequalities be before they become incompatible with human dignity and before they threaten the democratic system? In the second half of the 20th century, Rawls[233], Nozick[234] and Elster[235] made some of the most prominent contributions to our understanding of these issues of distributive justice and the moral status of inequality.

John Rawls is primarily concerned with establishing maxims of social justice. In order to do so, he starts from an imaginary "original position" in which people are placed. In this hypothetical situation, people do not have any knowledge about their talents, abilities and social status. Furthermore, Rawls assumes that these people are not aware of any particular purposes in life, but they only know that it will be useful to have various "primary goods", which, according to Rawls are "the principles that rational and free persons concerned to further their own interests would accept in an initial position of equality as defining the fundamentals of the terms of their association"[236]. Rawls lists these "primary goods" as rights and liberties, opportunities and powers, income and wealth and the bases of self-respect. According to Rawls, everyone wants as many of these "primary goods" as possible, but, because, in the "original position", "no one knows his place in society, his class position or social status, nor does anyone know his fortune in the distribution of natural assets and abilities, his intelligence, strength and the

233 John Rawls, *A Theory of Justice*, Revised edition, Cambridge, Mass.: Belknap Press, 1999 (originally published in 1971).

234 Robert Nozick, *Anarchy, State and Utopia*, New York: Basic Books, 1974.

235 Jon Elster, *Local Justice*, New York: Russeell Sage Foundation, 1992; J. Elster and K.O. Moene (eds), *Alternatives to Capitalism*, Cambridge: Cambridge University Press, 1989.

236 Rawls, *A Theory of Justice*, p. 11.

like"[237], people are constrained to put forward general distributive principles.

Rawls's first maxim of justice is the following: "each person is to have an equal right to the most extensive basic liberty compatible with a similar liberty for others"[238]. The basic liberties of citizens are political liberty (i.e., to vote and run for office), freedom of speech and assembly, liberty of conscience, freedom of thought, freedom of the person along with the right to hold private property, and freedom from arbitrary arrest. Within the framework of Rawls's philosophy, this maxim of justice is absolute and may never be violated, even for the sake of the second maxim, whereas various basic rights may be traded off against each other for the sake of establishing the optimal system of rights.

Rawls's second maxim of justice is the following: "social and economic inequalities are to be arranged so that they are both (a) reasonably expected to be to everyone's advantage, and (b) attached to positions and offices open to all"[239]. For instance, according this rationale, it is fair that a doctor makes more money than a porter, because, if this were not the case, people would not study and train to become doctors and there would be no medical care. Hence, the fact that a doctor makes more money than a porter benefits not only him but the entire society, including the porter, since, in this way, he can have medical care.

In his Tanner and Dewey lectures[240], Rawls has given further explanations about his theory of "justice as fairness". In particular, answering the criticism that his theory is indefensibly ahistorical, since it attempts to derive principles of justice entirely from general assumptions about human purposes, Rawls argued that his theory reflects the traditions of a modern democratic state. Moreover, an-

---

237 Ibid., p. 12.

238 Ibid., p. 60.

239 Ibid., p. 60.

240 John Rawls, "Kantian Constructivism in Moral Theory", *Journal of Philosophy*, Vol. 77, 1980, pp. 515-572 (The Dewey Lectures); John Rawls, "The Basic Liberties and their Priority", in S.M. McMurrin (ed.), *The Tanner Lectures on Human Values*, Salt Lake City: University of Utah Press, 1982, Vol. III.

swering the criticism that his notion of primary goods embodies an unwarranted individualism, Rawls argued that, in his theory, primary goods are to be understood in terms of a Kantian conception of the human subject as a moral agent that can follow public principles of justice and simultaneously devise and pursue its own ideals of good life.

Even though Rawls modified his original *Theory of Justice* in his Tanner and Dewey lectures, his theory still has two main defects:

(a) Rawls correctly tries to find a balance between the purpose of personal liberty — which is reflected in his first maxim of justice — and the purpose of social equality — which is reflected in his second maxim of justice. On the one hand, the quest for personal liberty expresses affirmation of life, in the sense that, as Albert Schweitzer has said, the individual consciousness deepens, makes more inward and exalts its will, and, as Nietzsche has said, man questions all doctrines that tend to drain life's expansive energies. On the other hand, the quest for social equality expresses people's concerns about the viability and sustainability of life. In other words, it is important to address the problem of how one will live his life more fully, and it is equally important to address the problem of how life will become more viable and more sustainable. The need to combine personal liberty with social equality urges us to follow a kairological approach, i.e., to solve this problem by applying the dialectic of kairicity, which I defined in Chapter 1. However, instead of following a kairological approach to the problem of justice, Rawls adopted a Kantian approach that 'contaminated' his theory of justice with the defects of Kant's moral rationalism that I mentioned earlier in this chapter.

(b) The second main defect of Rawls's theory is that, even though he tries to avoid the defects of utilitarianism through his "Kantian constructivism", his hypothesis about the "original position" is actually based on a form of utilitarianism, and, therefore, it makes his theory vulnerable to a criticism similar to the criticism of the general rationale of utilitarianism that I put forward earlier in this chapter.

A famous libertarian criticism of Rawls's theory of justice was put forward by Robert Nozick. Nozick objects to the maxim approach altogether, and, in particular, he argues that "to think that the task of a theory of distributive justice is to fill in the blank in 'to each according to his –', is to be predisposed to search for a pattern", but "no end-state principle or distributional pattern principle can be continuously realized without continuous interference in people's lives"[241]. Nozick proposes a 3-part "Entitlement Theory", according to which, in a just world, the following inductive definition would cover the entire subject of economic justice[242]: (a) Principle of justice in acquisition: If a person has acquired a holding in a just manner, then the given person is entitled to that holding. (b) Principle of justice in transfer: If a person has acquired a holding in accordance with the principle of justice in transfer, from someone else entitled to the holding, then the given person is entitled to the holding. (c) Principle of rectification of injustice: No one is entitled to a holding except by repeated applications of principles (a) and (b). Thus, entitlement implies that "a distribution is just if everyone is entitled to the holdings they possess under the distribution"[243]. But not everyone follows these rules: "some people steal from others, or defraud them, or enslave them, seizing their product and preventing them from living as they choose, or forcibly exclude others from competing in exchanges"[244]. Hence, Nozick argues, the principle of rectification of injustice is necessary.

Entitlement theory is based on John Locke's ideas about 'natural rights'. In fact, in the fifth chapter of his *Second Treatise on Government*, Locke formulates and defends the principle of justice in acqui-

---

241 Robert Nozick, "Distributive Justice", in J. Westphal (ed.), *Justice*, Indianapolis: Hackett Publishing Company, 1996, p. 17.
242 Nozick, *Anarchy, State and Utopia*, p. 151.
243 Ibid., p. 151.
244 Ibid., p. 152.

sition[245] and the principle of justice in transfer[246]. Nozick's entitlement theory is based on Nozick's self-ownership argument, which has been summarized by Will Kymlicka[247] as follows: (a) People own themselves. (b) The world is initially owned by nobody. (c) One can acquire absolute rights over a disproportionate share of the world, if he does not worsen the condition of others. (d) It is relatively easy to acquire absolute rights over a disproportionate share of the world. Therefore: (e) Given that private property has been appropriated, a free market in capital and labor is morally required.

The central argument of Nozick is that, because people own themselves and, therefore, their talents and productive abilities, they own whatever they can produce with those talents and productive abilities. Furthermore, Nozick stresses that, in a free market, one can sell the products of exercising his talents and productive abilities and that any taxation of the income from such selling "institute[s] (partial) ownership by others of people and their

---

245 John Locke, *Second Treatise on Government*, chapter 5, section 27: "Whatsoever then he removes out of the state that nature hath provided, and left it in, he hath mixed his labour with, and joined to it something that is his own, and thereby makes it his property. It being by him removed from the common state nature hath placed it in, it hath by this labour something annexed to it, that excludes the common right of other men: for this labour being the unquestionable property of the labourer, no man but he can have a right to what that is once joined to, at least where there is enough, and as good, left in common for others". For more details, see: John Colman, *John Locke's Moral Philosophy*, Edinburgh: Edinburgh University Press, 1983; C.B. Macpherson, *The Political Theory of Possessive Individualism*, Oxford: Oxford University Press, 1962.

246 John Locke, *Second Treatise on Government*, chapter 5, section 46: "Again, if he would give his nuts for a piece of metal, pleased with its colour; or exchange his sheep for shells, or wool for a sparkling pebble or a diamond, and keep those by him all his life, he invaded not the right of others; he might heap up as much of these durable things as he pleased; the exceeding of the bounds of his just property not lying in the largeness of his possession, but the perishing of any thing uselessly in it". For more details, see: Coleman, *John Locke's Moral Philosophy*; Macpherson, *The Political Theory of Possessive Individualism*.

247 Will Kymlicka, *Contemporary Political Philosophy*, Oxford: Clarendon Press, 1990, p. 112.

---

actions and labor"[248]. In this context, Nozick argues also that any system not legally recognizing the previous exclusive rights of ownership violates Kant's maxim to treat people always as ends in themselves and never merely as a means.

The three main defects of Nozick's theory are the following:

(a) Nozick uses the term 'self-ownership' in order to refer to the autonomy of the individual. However, he does not prove why self-ownership is only compatible with such strong property rights. In fact, self-ownership is equivalent to such strong property rights only if one assumes that his ownership of himself is equivalent to his ownership of the commodities that he produces and/ or purchases. But, if one assumes that his ownership of himself is equivalent to his ownership of the commodities that he produces and/ or purchases, then he reduces himself to a commodity. And if one reduces himself to a commodity, then on what grounds can he claim that he is superior to other commodities or that he owns other commodities in the name of a commodity (himself)?

(b) As I have already argued, in its attempt to assign meanings and significances to things, consciousness has the continuous tendency to move toward two directions — an extrinsic one and an intrinsic one — and the ego needs assistance from and cooperation with other egos. However, Nozick seems to ignore these things and to assume that the human being is characterized only by its autonomy, or self-ownership, as if it were an ontologically self-sufficient being. As I have already argued, every being is characterized not only by its autonomy but also by its participation in other beings, and, therefore, Nozick's principle of self-ownership fails to recognize what I have called the risk of under-information, which intensifies the inner ego at the expense of the social ego and leads to an ego-centric being. Therefore, there is no such thing as a pure individual.

(c) Nozick implicitly assumes that the economic history of autonomy constitutes the modern meaning of autonomy, but he does not make any attempt to show why every other interpretation of autonomy is wrong and that only the economic history of autono-

---

248 Nozick, *Anarchy, State and Utopia*, p. 172.

my gives us the true meaning of autonomy. Furthermore, Nozick's theory is not only incomplete, but it is also self-defeating. Nozick's argument of self-ownership does not lead to personal autonomy, but, instead, it eliminates personal autonomy and gives rise to a society that is determined by conformism and a complacent form of nihilism. Nozick's theory — by stressing that the establishment of a system of exclusive property rights is the best way of treating people with respect, as ends in themselves — is implicitly based on the idea that human beings came to the world primarily, if not only, in order to produce and consume commodities (economic goods/services). However, the true autonomy of the human being presupposes that human life has many meanings (and thus it is not exhausted in the production and consumption of commodities) and that human beings can set various goals about which they can argue that they are worth pursuing.

Jon Elster is a prominent representative of 'analytical Marxism' (an individualist reworking of Marx based on game theory) and 'methodological individualism'. Elster attempted to use analytical theories, and especially rational choice theory, in order to develop scientifically rigorous theories of economics and morality. According to Elster, "rational choice theory is far more than a technical tool for explaining behavior"; "it is also, and very importantly, a way of coming to grips with ourselves — not only what we should do, but even what we should be"[249]. He attempted to apply rational choice theory to politics, bias and constrained preferences, emotions, self-restraint and Marxism. Elster stressed that social-scientific explanations must be founded on 'methodological individualism' and 'microfoundations':

> By [methodological individualism] I mean the doctrine that all social phenomena — their structure and their change — are in principle explicable in ways that only involve individuals — their properties, their goals, their beliefs and their actions.[250]

---

249 Jon Elster, "Some Unresolved Problems in the Theory of Rational Behaviour", *Acta Sociologica*, Vol. 36, 1993, p. 179.

250 Jon Elster, *Making Sense of Marx*, Cambridge: Cambridge University Press, 1985, p. 5.

Hence, according to Elster, social phenomena should not be explained merely in terms of causal or functional regularities among social entities, but they should be explained primarily in terms of the mechanisms at the individual level ('microfoundations') by which the causal properties or functional norms of the social system are imposed on other social institutions and practices. Elster criticized Marxists and other social scientists for believing in functionalism, and he argued that Marxist explanations require microfoundations and that rational choice theory, and especially game theory, can provide such foundations.

According to Elster, rational choice is the outcome of a two-step process:

> To explain why a person in a given situation behaves in one way rather than in another, we can see his action as the result of two successive filtering processes. The first has the effect of limiting the set of abstractly possible actions to the feasible set, i.e., the set of actions that satisfy simultaneously a number of physical, technical, economic and politico-legal constraints. The second has the effect of singling out one member of the feasible set as the action which is to be carried out.[251]

Furthermore, Elster has put forward the following two arguments: (a) The optimal collection of information creates an infinite regress, in the sense that we have to collect information about how much information to collect about how much information to collect, etc. (b) It is often very difficult to estimate the marginal value of information because decision-making takes place in situations that are fast changing, unique or novel. According to Elster, the problem of choosing to change one's preferences or utility function cannot be reduced to a problem of utility maximization, but other rational considerations must find their explicit places in economic analysis.

In this context, Elster's theory of social choice and his approach to distributive justice are based on his assumption that preferences are endogenous to rational choice models. Elster is focused on the

---

251 Jon Elster, *Ulysses and the Sirens: Studies in Rationality and Irrationality*, Cambridge: Cambridge University Press, 1979, p. 76; Jon Elster, *Nuts and Bolts for the Social Sciences*, Cambridge: Cambridge University Press, 1989, pp. 13–14.

problem of endogenous preference change. He argues that individual preferences are formed through the process of political decision-making itself[252], and, therefore, individual preferences are not 'a priori' or exogenous. However, even though Elster correctly draws attention to the ways in which preferences are modified through the process of political decision-making itself, he fails to see that, at some point, during the process of political decision-making, individual preferences must be aggregated into a single social preference ranking, and this fact philosophically legitimates functionalism-structuralism. In other words, the fact that individual beliefs and preferences are affected by the process of political decision-making does not alter the fact that these beliefs and preferences must be aggregated into a consistent collective preference ranking. Hence, methodological individualism and functionalism can and should be considered as two components of a kairological methodology, which is capable of capturing the dialectical relationship between individuals and structures. Furthermore, as I have already argued, kairology enables us to overcome the defects and epistemological limits of rational choice theory. In fact, Elster himself (who started his research work with the ambition to, somehow, 'divinize' rational choice theory), in his later writings, admitted that rational choice theory is not as powerful as he had initially contended. A 1991 review in the *London Review of Books* noted that "Elster has lost his bearings, or at least his faith. [His latest book], he says, 'reflects an increasing disillusion with the power of reason'"[253]. In fact, in his book *Explaining Social Behavior*, Elster argues that

> I now believe that rational-choice theory has less explanatory power than I used to think. Do real people act on the calculations that make up many pages of mathematical appendixes in leading journals? I do not think so... *There is no general nonintentional mechanism that can simulate or mimic rationality...*At the same time, the empirical support...tends to be quite weak. This is of course a sweeping statement...let me simply point out the high level of disagreement among competent scholars...fundamental,

252 Jon Elster, "The Market and the Forum: Three Varieties of Political Theory", in J. Elster and A. Hyland (eds), *Foundations of Social Choice Theory*, Cambridge: Cambridge University Press, 1986, pp. 103–132.
253 Martin Hollis, "Why Elster is Stuck and Needs to Recover His Faith", *London Review of Books*, January 13, 1991.

persistent disagreements among 'schools'. We *never* observe the kind of many-decimal-points precision that would put controversy to rest.[254]

In the sequel, I shall defend a kairological approach to the issue of distributive justice in the field of economics. In Chapter 1, I presented kairology and I defended it as a general theory of human systems. In the light of the arguments that I have put forward until now, kairology implies the following two principles about justice and law:

(a) The idea of justice should not be identified with the idea of correct positive law. The idea of justice consists in a mean with regards to the rights and the duties of the social actors. On the other hand, the idea of correct positive law consists in the accumulation of various (and possibly mutually conflicting) legal principles into a system that is called a 'legal order' and aims at securing social peace and certainty with regards to the legal commitments that hold in a given society.

A non-kairological (i.e., 'uncritical' and deprived of discretion) attempt to pursue and apply justice may undermine the Legislature's attempt to pass correct legal rules. In other words, a non-kairological attempt to pursue and apply justice may lead to tragically unjust situations, as it is suggested by the sarcastic aphorism "fiat iustitia, pereat mundus"[255] (i.e., "let there be justice, though the world perish"), and, therefore, we must agree with Thomas Aquinas's assertion that "justitia sine misericordia crudelitas est"[256] (i.e., "justice without mercy is cruelty"). If justice is pursued and applied in a manner that is not in agreement with the dialectic of kairicity, which I defined in Chapter 1, then it ceases to express the principle of the mean and the political maxim of proportionality, which, according to Aristotle, constitute the essence of justice. Exactly be-

---

254 Jon Elster, *Explaining Social Behavior: More Nuts and Bolts for the Social Sciences*, Cambridge: Cambridge University Press, 2007, pp. 5, 25ff.

255 This statement was the motto of Ferdinand I, Holy Roman Emperor (1558), probably originating from Philipp Melanchthon's book *Loci Communes*.

256 See: Heinrich Henkel, *Introduction to the Philosophy of Right*, trans. G.E. Ordeig, Madrid: Taurus, 1968.

cause the principle of the mean and the political maxim of proportionality constitute the essence of justice, the very nature of justice excludes every kind of 'excess of justice'. The presence of excess signifies violation of the principle of the mean and of the political maxim of proportionality, and, therefore, it signifies injustice. In his *Great Ethics*, 1200a 17-30, Aristotle argues as follows:

> Such things as this too will no less raise a puzzle, whether it is ever with the virtues the way it is with the other goods (the external goods and the goods of the body). For when these go to excess they make people worse, for example when wealth is plentiful it makes people proud and nasty; and the same too with the other goods, rule, honor, beauty, size. Is virtue, then, also such that if someone has justice or courage to excess he will be worse? Or does it not say this? But from virtue comes honor, and honor, when it gets to be great, makes people worse. Virtue will as a result, it says, plainly make people worse as it advances further in amount (virtue is cause of honor, so that virtue too, as it becomes greater, would make people worse)... So neither honor nor rule will make the virtuous man worse, just as virtue will not either. But on the whole, since it was determined by us at the start that virtues are mean states and that the more the virtue the more it is a mean, the result is that far from making him worse as it progresses in amount virtue will make him better. For the mean was a mean of excess and want in the passions.

However, it should be mentioned that justice (even when it is pure from excess) is not always able to lead to the establishment of a correct legal order. Correct laws are not only dictated by the idea of justice, but they are also dictated by other fundamental principles. For instance, let us consider two laws, say X and Y. X may be more just than Y, but Y may be more correct than X, in the sense that Y may provide higher levels of legal certainty and of economic safety than X. Furthermore, the enforcement of a just and procedurally correct decision may cause the total financial collapse of a debtor, and, therefore, it may, ultimately, prove to cause worse results than those that could be caused by a less just decision.

(b) Positive law is determined by legal principles that must be evaluated and applied according to *ad hoc* criteria, on a case-by-case basis, by the legislative and the judicial authorities. Whereas positive law is determined by socially accepted legal principles, the choice among different mutually conflicting legal principles is not determined by the legal order itself[257]; this choice takes place according to the manner in which decision-makers conceive the 'supreme good', i.e., it is a question that belongs to the philosophy of morality.

---

257 See: H.L.A. Hart, *Law, Liberty, and Morality*, Stanford: Stanford University Press, 1963.

CHAPTER 13. KAIROLOGY AS A RESEARCH PROGRAM FOR PERSONAL AND SOCIAL AUTONOMY

By following the dialectic of kairicity, consciousness achieves its integration into the (external) world and the reconstruction and utilization of the world. Thus, ultimately, the world is formed in accordance with the intentionality of consciousness. This is the meaning of civilization and culture. As I have explained in previous books of mine[258], 'civilization' is a structure that consists of objectivations of the intentionality of human consciousness through technology and institutions, and 'culture' is a reflective attitude toward institutions and an attempt to transcend institutions through myth, whose complex structure reflects the structure of institutions ('myth' being the spiritual core of the elements of a civilization).

In the above-mentioned conceptual context, we can divide all forms of social organization (e.g. societies, markets, corporations, international organizations, etc.) into two general categories: kairic social organizations and non-kairic social organizations. In non-kairic social organizations, people unquestionably conform to the rules, values, goals of life and ways of life that the institutionalized social structure imposes on them and with which it spiritually nur-

---

258 See for instance: Laos, *Foundations of Cultural Diplomacy*.

tures them. For instance, for a classical Jew, e.g. a Jew of the era that is described in the Old Testament, the question whether the established legal system is just cannot be posed, in the sense that, for him, this question is meaningless, because, according to the classical Jewish culture, the Jewish law was given to Moses by God Himself. Moreover, a similar mentality characterizes all traditional Asian societies, pre-Colombian American societies, primitive races and the traditional medieval European societies.

On the other hand, in kairic social organizations, the fundamental issues of social life are essentially contested and reality is approached in terms of the dialectic of kairicity. The most characteristic examples of kairic societies are the ancient Athenian city-state from the 8th century BC to the 5th century BC and the Western European societies from the Late Middle Ages onwards. These societies subjected the fundamental issues of social organization to kairological study and management, gave birth to a movement of political awakening and participation that potentially included everybody, and allowed their citizens to question traditional representations of the world and traditional ideas about what has value and what has not, about what is just and what is not, etc.

One of the most important characteristics of the citizens of a kairic society is the fact that they pose themselves such questions as: 'how should society be institutionalized?', 'how should we think?', 'what is truth?', etc. Why is this characteristic of the citizens of a kairic society so important? Because it makes people aware of the fact that every society creates its institutions on the basis of values that orientate people's life and activity toward concrete institutions and acts. For instance, one of the values on the basis of which a society creates its institutions may be that of 'rationality'; however, the manner in which a kairic society understands this value is very different from the manner in which a non-kairic society understands the same fundamental value: a non-kairic society views 'rationality' as an absolute logical structure that is placed above and beyond any criticism, and, therefore, a non-kairic society is primarily characterized by routines, whereas a kairic society constantly subjects all the fundamental significations that underpin its institution to criticism, and, therefore, a kairic society is primarily characterized by creativity, innovation and freedom.

A kairic society chooses its values not in order to be enslaved to those values, or to a tradition, but because its values are characterized by kairicity and are susceptible to criticism. In other words, a kairic society lacks neither tradition nor values, but it refuses to accept all those traditions and values that are not characterized by kairicity and are not susceptible to criticism. A kairic society stresses the right and the ability of criticism neither as an end in itself nor as a pleasant habit, but as an expression of personal and social autonomy.

The creation of the first political community whose members wanted to undertake the responsibility of regulating their lives and their social relations and to become autonomous took place in ancient Greece. As we read in Thucydides's *Peloponnesian War*[259], Pericles (ca. 495-429 BC), one of the most prominent and influential statesmen and generals of Athens, argued that the institutional framework of Athens enabled its citizens to combine the care of their private affairs with a share of public life:

> An Athenian citizen does not neglect the state because he takes care of his own household; and even those of us who are engaged in business have a very fair idea of politics. We alone regard a man who takes no interest in public affairs, not as a harmless, but as a useless character; and if few of us are originators, we are all sound judges of policy.

Furthermore, according to Pericles, inextricably related to the previous principle of political participation is the principle that no man is born to office and no man buys office:

> When a citizen is in any way distinguished, he is preferred to the public service, not as a matter of privilege, but as the reward of merit. Neither is poverty a bar, but a man may benefit his country whatever be the obscurity of his condition.

In addition, Pericles argues that, in the Athenian political system, the principles of freedom and respect for law are united as follows:

---

259 Thucydides, *The Peloponnesian War*, trans. B. Jowett, Oxford: Clarendon Press, 1900 ("Funeral Oration of Pericles").

There is no exclusiveness in our public life, and in our private intercourse we are not suspicious of one another, nor angry with our neighbor if he does what he likes; we do not put on sour looks at him which, though harmless, are not pleasant. While we are thus unconstrained in our private intercourse, a spirit of reverence pervades our public acts; we are prevented from doing wrong by respect for the authorities and for the laws, having an especial regard to those who are ordained for the protection of the injured as well as to those unwritten laws which bring upon the transgressor of them the reprobation of the general sentiment.

Through the previous statement, Pericles displays the kairicity of the Athenian democracy. Finally, Pericles states that the activities of the city are based on the voluntary cooperation and on the critical thought of the citizens, and he displays the kairicity of the Athenians' public ethos as follows:

The great impediment to action is, in our opinion, not discussion, but the want of that knowledge which is gained by discussion preparatory to action. For we have a peculiar power of thinking before we act and of acting too, whereas other men are courageous from ignorance but hesitate upon reflection.

Even though the ancient Greek democratic system can be criticized on several grounds[260] (e.g. for being based on a narrow definition of the citizen body, for conducting elections via lottery, for not having lawyers, for being based on a much simpler economic system than the one which characterizes modern societies, etc) and even though it is not a model that should be copied as such by modern societies, it is an eternal source of democratic inspiration, since "the Athenian ideal might be summed up in a single phrase as the conception of free citizenship in a free state"[261].

Thomas Jefferson (1743–1826), the third President of the United States of America (1801–1809) and the writer of the Declaration of Independence, explained the meaning of personal and social autonomy within the framework of a democratic polity through the following statements: "I am not among those who fear the people. They, and not the rich, are our dependence for continued freedom"

260 Lynn Hunt et al., *The Challenge of the West*, Lexington, MA: D.C. Health & Company, 1995, pp. 66-69, 81-83.

261 G.H. Sabine and T.L. Thorson, *A History of Political Theory*, 4th edition, Florida: Holt, Rimehart and Winston, Inc., 1973, pp. 33.

(Thomas Jefferson to Samuel Kercheval, 1816). "No government can continue good, but under the control of the people" (Thomas Jefferson to John Adams, 1819). "I know no safe depository of the ultimate powers of the society but the people themselves; and if we think them not enlightened enough to exercise their control with a wholesome discretion, the remedy is not to take it from them, but to inform their discretion by education. This is the true corrective of abuses of constitutional power" (Thomas Jefferson to William C. Jarvis, 1820).

Marquis de Lafayette, leader of the "Garde national" during the French Revolution, stressed that: "True republicanism is the sovereignty of the people. There are natural and imprescriptible rights which an entire nation has no right to violate". In this context, Marquis de Lafayette explained the conditions under which revolution is justified: "When the government violates the people's rights, insurrection is, for the people and for each portion of the people, the most sacred of the rights and the most indispensable of duties". Jean-Paul Marat, one of the most influential journalists and politicians during the French Revolution, stressed that individual freedom and popular sovereignty cannot practically exist without each other: "To form a truly free constitution, that's to say, truly just and wise, the first point, the main point, the capital point, is that all the laws be agreed on by the people, after considered reflection, and especially having taken time to see what's at stake"[262].

Furthermore, it is important to mention that certain representatives of the modern labor movement[263] have played an important role in the promotion of the quest for personal and social autonomy. Victor Serge (1890–1947) is a characteristic example. According to

---

262 J.-P. Marat, "Letter to Camille Desmoulins", June 24, 1789.

263 One of the first and most influential manifestations of the labor movement was the "Chartist Movement". In 1836, the "Chartist Movement" was founded because workers realized that Parliament was so unrepresentative of their interests that it would have to be reformed. Hobsbawm writes that the Chartists' demands were: manhood suffrage, vote by ballot, equal electoral districts, payment of members of parliament, annual parliaments, and abolition of property qualification for (parliamentary) candidates; Eric Hobsbawm, *The Age of Revolution*, London: Pelican, 1962, pp. 144, 162.

Serge, the responsibility of free-thinking revolutionaries is "to proclaim by their criticism and activity that the crystallization of the workers' State must be avoided at all costs"[264], and he warned that "power exercises upon those who hold it a baleful influence which is often expressed in deplorable occupational perversions"[265]. Moreover, Bob Black has put forward the following intellectually challenging and thought-provoking arguments:

> [C]ommunism is the final fulfillment of individualism...The apparent contradiction between individualism and communism rests on a misunderstanding of both...Subjectivity is also objective: the individual really is subjective. It is nonsense to speak of 'emphatically prioritizing the social over the individual'...You may as well speak of prioritizing the chicken over the egg. Anarchy is a 'method of individualization'. It aims to combine the greatest individual development with the greatest communal unity.[266]

The conclusion that follows from the arguments that I have put forward in this chapter is that kairicity implies personal and social autonomy, and personal and social autonomy implies kairicity. In order to understand this conclusion, one must bear in mind that the term 'autonomy' comes from the Greek word 'autonomos', which has two roots: 'autos', which means 'self', and 'nomos', which means 'law'. In other words, the root 'autos' (self) stresses the element of individual freedom, and the root 'nomos' (law) stresses the fact that individual freedom does not mean arbitrary idealistic action, but it consists in the free and unbiased institution of a rational order (as opposed to chaos), which expresses the kairicity of consciousness. Thus, 'autonomy' does not mean 'anomy' (absence of law), but it means that men live by their *own* laws, i.e., by laws that express their kairic action. Therefore, autonomy is based on the dialectic of kairicity and is possible due to the kairic action of consciousness.

Kairicity implies that there is a dynamic continuity between the reality of the world and the reality of consciousness and that, due

---

264 Victor Serge, *Les Anarchistes et l'expérience de la révolution russe*, Paris: Bibliothèque du travail, 1921, p. 34.

265 Ibid., p. 34.

266 Bob Black, *Nightmares of Reason*, http://www.theanarchistlibrary.org
Moreover, see: Bob Black, *Anarchy after Leftism*, Columbia, MO: C.A.L. Press, 1997.

to this dynamic continuity, the intentionality of consciousness can reconstruct and utilize the world, and, therefore, consciousness can become its own legislator. Furthermore, the very fact that the 'self' needs laws — even if these laws are made by the 'self' — implies that autonomy is not an arbitrary idealistic activity and that it has nothing to do with uncontrolled volition. Therefore, autonomy can be achieved due to the kairicity of consciousness and can be pursued by following the dialectic of kairicity.

CHAPTER 14. KAIRICITY AND NETWORK SOCIETY

The term 'network society' was coined by the Dutch sociologist Jan van Dijk and the Spanish sociologist Manuel Castells. Van Dijk argues that:

> [W]ith little exaggeration, we may call the 21st century the age of networks. Networks are becoming the nervous system of our society, and we can expect this infrastructure to have more influence on entire social and personal lives than did the construction of roads for the transportation of goods and people in the past.[267]

Additionally, Jan van Dijk makes the following observations:

> Information and communication networks enable new types of combined vertical and horizontal control in organizations. Human supervision is replaced by the technical control of information systems. Infocracy takes the place of bureaucracy...Coordination is achieved by communication and knowledge networks. They have both horizontal and vertical characteristics. Horizontal are all kinds of cross-functional and virtual teams within and across organizational units, computer-supported collaborative work (CSCW) and so-called concurrent engineering (working in parallel instead of linearly). Vertical are identity and performance controls, personnel registration systems and password-protected databases.[268]

---

267 Jan van Dijk, *The Network Society*, 2nd edition, London: Sage, 2006, p. 2.
268 Ibid., p. 75.

According to Manuel Castells[269], the network society is characterized by the growing importance of social movements, and this growth will be built through two key channels. The first channel consists of the "media prophets", i.e., personalities who symbolize certain cultural values for a large group of people (e.g., the singer Sting campaigns for the preservation of rainforests). The second, and more subtle, channel consists of the multifaceted networks of social change. Castells argues that these social movements are responsible for the production and dissemination of new cultural codes and they may even give rise to new forms of social organization.

In fact, hand in hand with the development of network society goes the development of a new type of regulatory system known as "civil regulation". Bragd[270] has pointed out that, due to civil regulation, it becomes increasingly difficult for firms to justify their actions vis-à-vis the rest of society solely on the basis of covenants and other arrangements they have made with the government. If a firm behaves in a manner that is not acceptable to society at large, then the resulting criticism may damage its reputation, and, therefore, the continuity of its operation may be jeopardized. This risk is analogous to the velocity of the dissemination of adverse publicity by the media and over the internet. As Chris Marsden, former BP's Chairman, put it, "there is...a new form of global governance evolving that is made up of codes and accountability systems, which are becoming a kind of soft law"[271]. Thus, it is increasingly important for firms to communicate openly with "any group or individual who can affect or is affected by the achievement of an organization's purpose"[272].

---

269 Manuel Castells, *The Information Age: Economy, Society and Culture*, Oxford: Blackwell, 1997.

270 Annica Bragd et al., "Beyond Greening: New Dialogue and New Approaches for Developing Sustainability", *Business Strategy and the Environment*, Vol. 7, 1998, pp. 179–192.

271 Quoted in: Jem Bendell, "Civil Regulation: A New Form of Democratic Governance for the Global Economy?", in J. Bendell (ed.), *Terms of Endearment: Business, NGOs and Sustainable Development*, Sheffield: Greenleaf Publishing, 2000, pp. 239-254.

272 R.E. Freeman, *Strategic Management: A Stakeholder Approach*, Boston: Pitman, 1984, p. 52.

The need for open communication is highlighted by the fact that, in the era of advanced modernity, societies are increasingly preoccupied with hazards and insecurities induced and introduced by modernization itself, and, therefore, according to Ulrich Beck's terminology, they are "risk societies"[273]. All judgments of scientific and technological risks are related to values, especially when risks are associated with complex issues, such as those referring to the natural environment and to genetic engineering. Beck has made the following observations:

> These revived questions — what is humankind? what do we think about nature? — may be shunted back and forth between everyday life, politics and science. In the most advanced developmental stage of civilization they once again occupy a very high place on the agenda, even or *especially* where they were supposed to have been made invisible by their traditional magic cap of mathematical formulas and methodological controversies. Determinations of risks are the form in which ethics, and with it also philosophy, culture and politics, is resurrected *inside* the centers of modernization — in business, the natural sciences and the technical disciplines.[274]

As a result, no organization can afford to have blind faith in the efficiency and power of those who occupy the apex of the pyramid of the formal system of social organization and in the findings of scientific research; they also need to obtain approval of their conduct from an ever-expanding, multifaceted group of stakeholders[275].

As the number of the members of a network increases, the nonlinearities that characterize the behavior of the given network become more complex, and, therefore, the possibilities of personal choice become more significant, since the number of players increases. In other words, the impact of individual action increases. On the other hand, as networking increases, the opposite outcome may be produced — namely, the restrictions/ norms of collective over-organization may eliminate the personal ability to make indi-

---

273 Ulrich Beck, *Risk Society: Towards a New Modernity*, London: Sage, 1992.
274 Ibid., p. 28.
275 Cheryl Rodgers, "Making It Legit: New Ways of Generating Corporate Legitimacy in a Globalising World", in J. Bendell (ed.), *Terms of Endearment: Business, NGOs and Sustainable Development*, Sheffield: Greenleaf Publishing, 2000, pp. 40-48.

vidual choices. For instance, Prigogine and Herman[276] have studied vehicular traffic and discovered that, when the level of traffic density is low, then every driver behaves almost as he himself chooses, i.e., there is an "individual regime", but, as traffic becomes more and more dense, everyone pushes everyone else and is pushed by everyone else, i.e., there emerges a "collective regime". However, as traffic becomes more and more dense, the potential impact of an individual driver's decision to act in a non-conformist manner increases, e.g. a single driver can cause massive pile-up. In general, if the level of networking becomes extremely high, it may lead to phenomena of massive conformism, because everyone is strongly affected/ restricted by everyone else, and, therefore, it may undermine human creativity, but, on the other hand, in such a situation, the decision of an individual player or a small group of players to exhibit anti-conformist behavior can have a big impact on the network.

The challenges of network society imply that it is necessary to follow the dialectic of kairicity in order to create a sustainable social-economic system. Increased networking does not necessarily entail the elimination of individual responsibility and creativity. Given that, as I stressed in Chapter 13, the human being is the ultimate legislator of itself and that the human society is the ultimate legislator of itself, too, i.e., given that every structure that regulates human life is essentially dependent on human consciousness, the human being is always responsible for its life. And, as I argued in Chapter 1, the dialectic of kairicity is the most efficient manner in which the human being can take responsibility for its life.

Kairological economics does not aim at imposing a specific regulation of economic behavior, but it aims at securing the rights and at enhancing the abilities of the human beings to make kairic decisions, approaching political economy with an open and alert mind and with anthropocentric principles. A kairic person and a kairic society live at the edge of order (or at the edge of chaos), because they organize their lives in a manner that combines certainty and uncertainty, regulation and freedom, stability and change into a dy-

---

276 Ilia Prigogine and Robert Herman, *Kinetic Theory and Vehicular Traffic*, New York: Elsevier, 1971.

namic whole that reflects the kairicity of the human consciousness. Thus, from a certain viewpoint, kairological economics represents a continuous revolution in the field of political economy.

Chapter 15. Institutions And Economic Activity

In Chapter 13, I stressed that the human being is the ultimate legislator of itself and that the human society is the ultimate legislator of itself, too, in accordance with the kairicity of consciousness. Therefore, every social structure, including economic markets, is derived from the interaction of three categories of forces: (i) significations-values, (ii) institutions and (iii) economic resources (technological and organizational capabilities, natural resources, stocks of equipment — e.g. industries — and the wealth that can command these).

Institutional economics consists in the methical study of the role of institutions in shaping economic behavior. The origins of institutional economics can be traced back to the research work of Thorstein Veblen, who argued that there is a sharp distinction between technology and the "ceremonial sphere"[277], i.e., between instrumental and ceremonial functions. However, the name and the

---

277 The idea of Veblen as the originator of the technology-ceremonial dichotomy has been challenged by: G.M. Hodgson, "Dichotomizing the Dichotomy: Veblen versus Ayres", in S. Fayazmanesh and M.R. Tool (eds), *Institutionalist Method and Value: Essays in Honour of Paul Dale Bush*, Cheltenham: Edward Elgar, 1998, Vol. I, pp. 48-73; M. Rutherford, "Clarence Ayres and the Institutionalist Theory of Value", *Journal of*

core elements of institutional economics are originally due to Walton H. Hamilton[278]. In particular, Hamilton argues as follows:

> An appeal for 'institutional economics' implies no attack upon the truth or value of other bodies of economic thought, but it is a denial of the claims of other systems of thought to be 'economic theory'...*The proper subject-matter of economic theory is institutions.* The demand that economic theory relate to institutions is implicit in the plea for its relevancy. If it is to be germane to the problem of control it must relate to changeable elements of life and the agencies through which they are to be directed. Such elements of life and directive agencies are alike institutions. Control is exercised by modifying the arrangements which make up our scheme of economic life in such a way as better to satisfy our needs or our whims. Control is exercised through peculiar agencies which we have at hand.[279]

Moreover, the interplay between law and economics has been a major issue since the publication of the *Legal Foundations of Capitalism* by John R. Commons in 1924. Commons argues as follows:

> Legal theory and economic theory, in modern times, have based their explanations on Newton's principle of mechanism, then on Malthus' principle of scarcity, then on juristic principles of common rules that both limit and enlarge the field for individual wills in a world of mechanical forces and scarcity of resources. Since transactions are the economic units, and working rules are the principles on which the Supreme Court of the United States has been working over its theories of property, sovereignty and value, and since that court occupies the unique position of the first authoritative faculty of political economy in the world's history, we shall begin with the court's theory of property, liberty and value.[280]

A significant variant of 'institutional economics' is the so-called 'new institutional economics', which was developed in the late 20th century as an attempt to integrate later developments of neoclas-

---

Economic Issues, Vol. 15, 1981, pp. 657-674. Kairology challenges Veblen's technology-ceremonial dichotomy, too.

278 W.H. Hamilton, "The Institutional Approach to Economic Theory", *American Economic Review*, Vol. 9, 1919, pp. 309-318. Additionally, see: D.R. Scott, "Veblen Not an Institutional Economist", *American Economic Review*, Vol. 23, 1933, pp. 274-277.

279 Hamilton, "The Institutional Approach to Economic Theory", pp. 309, 313.

280 J.R. Commons, *Legal Foundations of Capitalism*, with a new introduction by J.E. Biddle and W.J. Samuels, New Jersey: Transaction Publishers, 2007 (originally published in 1924), p. 7.

---

sical economics into institutional economics. The origins of new institutional economics can be traced back to two research papers by Ronald Coase[281] (who received the Nobel Prize in Economics in 1991): "The Nature of the Firm" (1937) and "The Problem of Social Cost" (1960). In the latter research paper, Coase formulated the well-known Coase Theorem, which can be stated and explained in the following (equivalent) ways:

(a) "If one assumes rationality, no transaction costs, and no legal impediments to bargaining, *all* misallocations of resources would be fully cured in the market by bargains".[282]

(b) "In a world of perfect competition, perfect information, and zero transaction costs, the allocation of resources in the economy will be efficient and will be unaffected by legal rules regarding the initial impact of costs resulting from externalities".[283]

(c) "If transaction costs are zero the structure of the law does not matter because efficiency will result in any case".[284]

(d) "In a world of zero transaction costs, the allocation of resources will be efficient, and invariant with respect to legal rules of liability, income effects aside".[285]

(e) "A change in a liability rule will leave the agents' production and consumption decisions both unchanged and economically efficient within the following (implicit) framework: (a) two agents to each externality bargain, (b) perfect knowledge of one another's (convex) production and profit or utility functions, (c) competitive markets, (d) zero transactions costs, (e) costless court system,

---

281 Ronald Coase, "The Nature of the Firm", *Economica*, Vol. 4, 1937, pp. 368-405; Ronald Coase, "The Problem of Social Cost", *Journal of Law and Economics*, Vol. 3, 1960, pp. 1-44.

282 Guido Calabresi, "Transaction Costs, Resource Allocation and Liability Rules: A Comment", *Journal of Law and Economics*, Vol. 11, 1968, pp. 67-73.

283 D.H. Regan (1972), "The Problem of Social Cost Revisited", *Journal of Law and Economics*, Vol. 15, 1972, pp. 427-437.

284 A.M. Polinsky, "Economic Analysis as a Potentially Defective Product: A Buyer's Guide to Posner's Economic Analysis of Law", *Harvard Law Review*, Vol. 87, 1974, pp. 1655-1681.

285 R.O. Zerbe, Jr, "The Problem of Social Cost in Retrospect", *Research in Law and Economics*, Vol. 2, 1980, pp. 83-102.

(f) profit-maximizing producers and expected utility maximizing consumers, (g) no wealth effects, (h) agents will strike mutually advantageous bargains in the absence of transactions costs".[286]

The term 'new institutional economics' was coined by Oliver Williamson[287], who received the Nobel Prize in Economics in 2009. Williamson argues that the following factors cause 'free-market' failures that lead to the need and existence of hierarchies and organizations to mediate and economize transaction costs: (a) Bounded rationality and uncertainty/ complexity: internal organizations become necessary when actors characterized by bounded rationality are amidst a complex and uncertain environment. In internal organizations, exchange codes may secure a higher level of confidence and people have less risk of being disadvantaged by opportunism. (b) Opportunism and small numbers: Opportunism allows for strategic thinking, and, because of opportunism, one cannot trust everybody. Hence, agreements need to be monitored during execution, and, for this reason, a form of organization is necessary. Additionally, even though, at least theoretically, with large numbers of exchangers, one could avoid those who exhibit an aggressive opportunistic behavior (and thus punish them), in a market in which there is a small number of exchangers, the players who exhibit an aggressive opportunistic behavior cannot be easily avoided. (c) Information impactedness: "A derivative condition that arises mainly because of uncertainty and opportunism, though bounded rationality is involved as well. It exists when true underlying circumstances relevant to the transaction, or related set of transactions, are known to one or more parties but cannot be costlessly discerned by or displayed for others"[288]. Internal organizations serve to inhibit aggressive opportunism in situations of information disadvantage. (d) Atmosphere (interaction effects): Societal factors (e.g. loyalty, reciprocity, etc.) can affect transactions. Hence, certain modes of

---

286 E. Hoffman and M.L. Spitzer, "The Coase Theorem: Some Experimental Tests", *Journal of Law and Economics*, Vol. 25, 1982, pp. 73-98.

287 O.E. Williamson, *Markets and Hierarchies: Analysis and Antitrust Implications*, New York: Free Press, 1975.

288 Ibid., p. 31.

transaction may be rejected in some organizations if they are judged to be incompatible with the given organizations' value systems.

Douglass North[289], one of the most prominent economists associated with the research program of new institutional economics, has argued that institutions have three dimensions: formal rules, informal constraints, and enforcement mechanisms. Informal constraints come from socially transmitted information and are part of culture[290]. Formal constraints may increase the effectiveness of informal constraints, modify them, or supersede them[291]. Additionally, there are costs associated with imperfect enforcement because of costs associated with measuring contract compliance and because of costs associated with the fact that enforcement agents have their own utility functions[292]. Thus, according to North, the inability of societies to develop effective, low-cost enforcement of contracts causes economic stagnation. Furthermore, North has argued that the difference between the terms 'institution' and 'organization' should be based on the following definition: 'organizations' are purposeful entities endowed with governance arrangements that are created by their designers in order to coordinate team action and maximize their objectives defined by the opportunities afforded by the established institutional framework[293]. On the other hand, as I have already mentioned, according to North, 'institutions' are composed of formal rules, informal constraints, and enforcement mechanisms and determine the incentives for the kinds of knowledge and skills that pay off[294].

Following a rationale that is derived from the fundamental assumptions of rational choice theory, North argues that organizations change institutions at the margins whenever changing an institution is more profitable than investing in existing constraints. The rationality postulate allows one to extract conclusions about

289 D.C. North, *Institutions, Institutional Change and Economic Performance*, Cambridge: Cambridge University Press, 1990.
290 Ibid., p. 37.
291 Ibid., p. 46.
292 Ibid., pp. 54-57.
293 Ibid., p. 73.
294 Ibid., p. 78.

the behavior of economic actors exclusively from the knowledge of the system's structure. But, as I have already argued and as it has been shown by behavioral finance, if one is restricted to the analysis of structural causes, then he can easily find himself in the realm of pure theory. Moreover, as I have already argued, an institution is an objectivation of the intentionality, and especially of the kairicity, of consciousness, and, therefore, the entire spectrum of the values and ultimate goals of the actors must explicitly find its place in every operationally significant analysis of the dynamics of social organization.

Every social organization and every society, in general, operate in accordance with the dialectic of kairicity, but they are not always aware of this fact. Thus, when it ceases to be aware of its kairicity, an organization lapses into conformism and becomes alienated within the very institutions that the given organization has created, simply because it does not know any more, or because it does not dare to know, that institutions are consequences of the actors' kairic action. Thus, various social organizations and whole societies follow mythological approaches to institutions that teach that institutions are not consequences of the actors' kairic action and that they are derived from 'elsewhere', e.g. from God, from nature, from an absolute, closed logical system, etc. On the other hand, a kairic society is a society that knows the dynamic continuity between the reality of consciousness and the reality of the world, and its members creatively undertake the responsibility to make laws for themselves, thus allowing themselves to exist as autonomous persons, in accordance with the dialectic of kairicity. Furthermore, within the framework of a kairic society, a law is respectable because (and to the extent that) it is a manifestation of the kairicity of the human being and not because it is assumed to be derived from a reality that is independent of human consciousness.

Institutional economics, including the 'school' of new institutional economics, expresses a tendency of the modern economic thought to transcend the 'physiocratic fallacy' (I shall return to this term in Chapter 17) and to show that the intentionality of consciousness creates the economic order, but it ultimately succumbs to the core rationale of physiocracy, since institutional economics (including new institutional economics) remains intellectually anchored in a Newtonian conception of reality and in a utilitarian approach to human behavior that do not help the modern economist to understand the indeterminacy and relativity of social organization, the dynamics of the refutability of scientific propositions, and methodological nominalism.

A kairic institutional system necessarily aims for the establishment of an economic order that has the following characteristics: (i) it gives priority to personal and social autonomy; (ii) it allows the social actors to experience and realize the indeterminate dynamics of personal societal relations through the dialectic of kairicity; (iii) it understands the material world not as a neutral object but as a structure of logical qualities.

Chapter 16. The Eurozone, Totemism And Democratic Deficit

The Euro was adopted as the single legal tender of the Eurozone member states in 2002. The Treaty of Maastricht (signed on February 7, 1992) envisioned the introduction of a common currency in order to solve the problem of exchange rate instability among the currencies of the member states and to establish a central monetary authority controlling the European Union's money supply. Under such a monetary regime, market interest rates are expected to be equalized across boundaries, allowing only minor regional variations and differentials due to the risk rating and fiscal treatment of the various different financial instruments. In effect, the designers of the Economic and Monetary Union (EMU) of the European Union contemplated a regime similar to the Federal Reserve central banking structure in the U.S., with national central banks playing the role of the regional Federal Reserve Banks.

Within the framework of the EMU, open market and foreign exchange operations are carried out by the European Central Bank (ECB), subject to policy determinations by a board on which the national central banks are represented. The ECB is "autonomous" with a very clear cut mandate, focusing exclusively on price stability. Thus, this regime imposes a central monetary policy on all member states. However, the Treaty of Maastricht did not make provisions for the harmonization of other elements of effective economic integration.

What is different in the Eurozone context versus that of the U.S. is the lack of central fiscal policy, the lack of effective labor mobility, and the lack of the spirit of free creativity that inspires and motivates many players in the U.S. economic system. Of course, formally, in the Eurozone, labor is free to move, but cultural factors and the 'hospitality', or 'ambience', of the receiving region create substantial barriers, which deny effective labor mobility to the Eurozone. Moreover, even though the lack of central fiscal policy is partially compensated by the regional development policies of the EU, the latter do not serve a contra-cyclical purpose, and, in general, the resources commanded by the fiscal arm of the Eurozone are very meager in comparison to those of the member states.

The European Commission has argued that it is necessary to have a single currency if there is to be a successful single market. Among those disputing this claim is the former president of the German Bundesbank, Helmut Schlesinger, who in a speech in Los Angeles in April 1993, said the following:

> Many economists feel that the single European market will only have been completed economically if Europe actually also has a single currency. Nothing expresses this conviction better than the well known slogan, 'one market, one money'. However, I believe it to be somewhat short-sighted simply to regard the European monetary union as the logical conclusion to the process of economic integration. The monetary union is rather a step with a significance of its very own. A single market can exist and be beneficial without inevitably requiring further moves towards integration in the monetary sphere. Nobody to my knowledge is calling for the creation of a single North American currency, as the consequential establishment of a North American free trade area.[295]

In the same spirit, Martin Feldstein, Professor of Economics at Harvard and former chairman of the Council of Economic Advisers, predicted in June 1992 that:

---

295 Helmut Schlesinger, Speech in Los Angeles, April 16, 1993. See: http://www.brugesgroup.com

Monetary union is not needed to achieve the advantages of a free trade zone. On the contrary, an artificially contrived monetary union might actually reduce the volume of trade, and would almost certainly increase the level of unemployment.[296]

Hans Tietmeyer, former Bundesbank President, in a speech in Berlin on September 9, 1994, argued that:

Stable exchange rates cannot be determined by government ordinance or fixed arbitrarily by policy makers. Ultimately, durably fixed exchange rates are possible only in cases where economic performance is sufficiently convergent and economic policies have identical aims and models. In recent years, Europe has had to experience yet again how much damage can be done by fixing exchange rates in the absence of due convergence between economies if the fixed exchange rate has to be defended by unlimited central bank intervention.[297]

Additionally, on January 31, 1995, Eddie George, former Governor of the Bank of England, argued that:

It seems quite possible that a part of the answer to the widely differing levels of structural unemployment will need to be relative real wage adjustment. It is hard to imagine that this could be brought about through a reduction in nominal wages in the high unemployment countries, and without that it is possible that there would be a need for exchange rate adjustment to help bring about a real wage adjustment. Inadequate conversion would be likely to mean slower growth and higher or rapidly rising unemployment in some countries than in others. In that case, the imbalances could only be addressed through some combination of three possible adjustment mechanisms: one, long-term stagnation and unemployment in some parts of the monetary union; two, migration; three, fiscal transfers to the higher unemployment countries. None of these mechanisms appears particularly attractive, and if the tension were substantial then they could become politically divisive. The important thing is that we should recognise the economic significance of monetary union and debate the economic issues dispassionately.[298]

From a certain viewpoint, one can argue that significant benefits[299] are likely to accrue upon successful integration for Eurozone

---

296 Martin Feldstein, The Economist, June 13, 1992.

297 Hans Tietmeyer, Speech in Berlin, September 9, 1994. See: http://www.brugesgroup.com

298 Eddie George, Speech, January 31, 1995. See: http://www.brugesgroup.com

299 Such benefits include: exchange rate risk and the cost associated with it are eliminated in the Eurozone, the financial and economic man-

member states. But it should be pointed out that these benefits are mainly related to the interests of business and political elites. Furthermore, in the context of the EMU system that was established by the Maastricht Treaty, the most significant macroeconomic problem arises when a tight monetary policy is adopted by the ECB in the face of, or causing, substantial economic dislocation and unemployment in certain regions of the Eurozone. Given the ECB's "independence" and given that the Maastricht Treaty does not make any provisions about fiscal stabilization instruments in the Eurozone, problems of regional imbalance cannot be addressed in an institutional manner by national representatives in the governing apparatus of the European Union. The Eurozone is not only undemocratic and inefficient, but additionally it operates as an instrument for the realization and promotion of the dominance of Germany over the Eurozone, given that Germany is the strongest player in the Eurozone and also it is the largest creditor nation with the best sovereign credit. As former British Prime Minister Margaret Thatcher had correctly forecasted and stressed in the 1990s, when she was bravely fighting against Jacques Delors's model of EMU, Germany would be phobic about inflation, while the Euro would prove fatal to the poor member states of the Eurozone and it would devastate their inefficient economies.

Furthermore, Germany's policy of relying on exports for growth and of maintaining a high household savings rate and a low level of consumption destabilizes the Eurozone and, in effect, utilizes the rigid economic regime of the Eurozone in order to promote the national interests of Germany at a cost to other member states. For instance, a trade surplus for Germany with Greece necessitates a trade deficit for Greece with Germany. Thus, Germany's trade policy has a very negative impact on its Eurozone trade partners (since the latter cannot resolve their problems through currency flexibility), and, by limiting wage growth over the decade of the 2000s, Germany practically followed a policy of devaluation against its

---

agement for the firms is simplified with the replacement of national currencies by the Euro, price comparisons are facilitated, competition among firms is intensified, etc.

Eurozone partners. On the other hand, the weaker economies of the Eurozone could not deflate wages to regain their competitiveness with Germany without creating a deflationary slump[300].

However, the EMU system that was established by the Maastricht Treaty is not only an instrument through which Germany pursues its domination over the Eurozone, but also it is a system that serves the interests of a business and especially banking elite. In particular, it is a totemic society whose 'totem' is the rationalistic and bureaucratic economic system that was established by the Maastricht Treaty, whose 'priesthood' is the European Central Bank, and whose 'Holy Inquisition' is an army of technocrats who are always willing to rationalize and impose a pan-European conformism to the 'Bulls' of the Eurozone's business and banking elite. Furthermore, Jean-Jacques Rosa, who served as an economic adviser to the French Prime Minister during 1997–1999 and is the founder of the MBA program and two doctoral programs at the Institute of Political Studies in Paris, has explained in the detail the manner in which "European politicians and businessmen decided to circumvent democratic consent in order to lock their societies into a single European super-state"[301].

It should be pointed out that it is one thing to argue that the central monetary authority should be independent of political control on a routine basis, but it is completely another that the central monetary authority can function for long irrespective of a strong political consensus on the contrary[302]. The Maastricht Treaty estab-

---

300 See for instance: Martin Wolf, "Why Germany Cannot Be a Model for the Eurozone", *Financial Times*, March 30, 2010.

301 Jean-Jacques Rosa, *Euro Exit: Why (and How) to Get Rid of the Monetary Union*, New York: Algora Publishing, 2012.

302 In June 1990, as an alternative to European Commission President Delors's proposal for a single currency and European bank, British Chancellor John Major proposed a new European currency that would circulate alongside national currencies, thus allowing European economies to be integrated into a single monetary zone only when they would be really ready to do so, i.e., when they would have converged to the lowest levels of unemployment and inflation. According to Major, this European currency, which he called the "hard ECU", would be used initially by businesses and tourists, and managed by a new European

lishes rules of operation of the Eurozone that are rigid and reflect the monolithic point of view of the Germans, the Austrians and the Dutch, thus giving rise to a giant bureaucratic and authoritarian structure that is unable to endorse the dialectic of kairicity. On the other hand, due to the kairicity that characterizes the traditional American mentality, even though American states are required by their constitutions to maintain a "balanced" budget, many American states accomplish this attenuation by defining the term 'budget' narrowly, so that it refers only to expenditures for "current" purposes, opening up the possibility that expenditures need not be balanced by revenues. A 'capital project' is, by definition, one that yields benefits over a much wider horizon than the expenditure horizon. For instance, the so-called infrastructure investments yield benefits over a long period by improving the general productivity characteristics of the economy, and, for this reason, they are excluded from the requirement that they be matched by current revenues (hence, they may be financed by deficits and consequent borrowing from the global capital market). After all, it is unreasonable to ask the current set of taxpayers to pay for the bulk of expenditures that will continue to yield benefits to future generations, and it is equally unreasonable to refuse to finance useful infrastructure investments through borrowed funds.

The monolithic point of view of the Germans, the Austrians and the Dutch deprives the Eurozone of the elements of creativity and democracy, which are necessary presuppositions of development, and, through rigid bureaucracies and high taxation of the lower and the middle classes, the Eurozone promotes the concentration of capital in the hands of a corporate and banking elite and tends to transform the lower and the middle classes (i.e., the backbone of the 'civil system') into a kind of serfs of a corporate and banking pan-European elite, thus restoring a medieval economic ethos. The

---

monetary fund. Major said: "What we're seeking to do is to provide a currency that those who wish to use it could use, either for business transactions or personal transactions, without going down the route of a single currency across the whole of Europe, which we think has enormous difficulties and enormous dangers too"; see: http://news.bbc.co.uk

first nine years of the operation of the Euro and the Eurozone financial crisis of 2010-2011 made clear that, unless the European Union adopts a policy based on discretion, democratic accountability and creativity, i.e., unless it adopts a policy based on the dialectic of kairicity, it will be a degenerate form of union of European peoples and a liberal oligarchy, which is not even a caricature of the original ideal of European unity that was envisaged by William Penn (1644 –1718), Jean Omer Marie Gabriel Monnet (1888–1979), Paul Valéry (1871–1945), etc.

CHAPTER 17. PHILOSOPHY OF HISTORY AND COMPARATIVE ECONOMICS

The dialectic of kairicity implies that history is the fullest expression of human creativity. The discontinuity that is caused by the kairic action of humanity does not completely abolish the continuity of historical becoming, but, instead, the continuity of historical becoming is restructured by the imposition of human intentionality upon time. Thus, instead of being defeated by historical necessities, the human being, due to its ability to restructure the reality of the world through the kairicity of human consciousness, transcends the necessity that characterizes the natural world and becomes the creator and the manager of human destiny.

From the above-mentioned standpoint, the philosophy of history that underpins classical and neoclassical political economy expresses an ontological self-degradation of man. As I have already argued, these economic schools are heavily influenced by what I call the 'physiocratic fallacy'. In this chapter, I explain the meaning of the physiocratic fallacy in the context of different schools of economic thought.

The physiocratic fallacy in the context of the market economy: In this case, the physiocratic fallacy consists in an attempt to identify and explain the 'natural' social-economic order. By characterizing the system of laissez-faire capitalism as 'natural', the physiocrats as well as those classical and neoclassical economists who have followed their rationale attempt to present the logic that characterizes their economic theory as the only correct logic for the organization of social-economic life. The rationale of the physiocrats and of those classical and neoclassical economists who have followed their path has been summarized by Gunnar Myrdal as follows:

> Like all their contemporaries, the Physiocrats tried to interpret the 'natural order' of human society...they...looked upon the existing order as a fairly close approximation to this ideal natural order. It only had to be freed from the mutilating fetters of government intervention...their political ideal turned out to represent a theoretical abstraction which proved useful for dealing with problems of positive economics...In the framework of the natural order events were viewed as causally connected. The interests of individuals gave direction and cohesion to economic life, just as the force of gravitation held the planetary system together, an analogy which was popular at the time. Probably inspired by the idea of the social contract, the Physiocrats represented the 'circular' flow of economic life as a series of exchanges between individuals and classes...In the course of time the physiocratic analysis of 'natural' price formation became even more fruitful by being linked with the idea of equilibrium... Adam Smith fairly consistently identified natural price and normal price. Later stages in the development of this doctrine were Walras's *equilibre general*, Marshall's theory of normal price, and J.B. Clark's theory of static and atomistic price formation. The concept of equilibrium...was taken over from the natural sciences...[303]

However, the physiocrats and their supporters never explained why 'nature' must take ontological precedence over 'hypostasis' or 'personhood'. 'Hypostasis' means the existence of an individual substance in itself, whereas nature as a species is a common thing, which is predicated of hypostases and has its existence in them, and, thus, hypostasis not only possesses common as well as individual characteristics of the subject, but also exists in itself, whereas nature does not exist in itself, but is to be found in hypostasis. Thus, each and every human being, having a hypostatic form of existence, is not the same as the abstract concept of 'humanity', but

303 Gunnar Myrdal, *The Political Element in the Development of Economic Theory*, London: Routledge & Kegan Paul, 1953, pp. 31-32.

it is characterized by an existential 'otherness', i.e., it substantiates the human nature in a unique, personal manner. In fact, the essence of 'individualism' — which is strongly praised by the supporters of laissez-faire capitalism — consists in the hypostatic form of existence of the human being. Therefore, the physiocratic attempt to reduce individualism to the 'natural order of human organization', instead of interpreting individualism as a consequence of the hypostatic form of human existence, is a blatant antinomy. This blatant antinomy pervades the foundations of classical and neoclassical economics.

The idealized world of neoclassical economics — which is the 'orthodoxy' of modern political economy — provides a defence for the marginalization and methodical undermining of personal autonomy within market economies, since the latter are based on the postulation of laws that are deemed beyond critique (because they are viewed as 'natural'). According to the physiocratic fallacy, these laws are claimed to be 'scientific' owing to their supposed basis in observation of the reality of the external world and the application of logically consistent mathematical models. By giving prime importance to rational mastery as shaping the political and cultural arrangements in any given society, neoclassical economics, ultimately, marginalizes and methodically undermines individual liberty.

Furthermore, the foundations of classical and neoclassical economics ignore the dynamic continuity between the reality of the world and the reality of consciousness, which I emphasize throughout this book.

The physiocratic fallacy in the context of Marxism: In this case, the physiocratic fallacy consists in an attempt to discover the forces that drive historical change independently of human consciousness, as if they were natural laws. In his book *The Capital*, Vol. III, Karl Marx defends the freedom of man as follows:

> In fact, the realm of freedom actually begins only where labour which is determined by necessity and mundane considerations ceases; thus in the very nature of things it lies beyond the sphere of actual material production. Just as the savage must wrestle with Nature to satisfy his wants, to maintain and reproduce

life, so must civilised man, and he must do so in all social for-
mations and under all possible modes of production. With his
development this realm of physical necessity expands as a result of his wants; but, at the same time, the forces of production
which satisfy these wants also increase. Freedom in this field
can only consist in socialised man, the associated producers,
rationally regulating their interchange with Nature, bringing
it under their common control, instead of being ruled by it as
by the blind forces of Nature; and achieving this with the least
expenditure of energy and under conditions most favourable to,
and worthy of, their human nature.[304]

But, even though Marx has declared the overthrow of the civil
social order through the action of the working class, he has also argued that the proletariat revolution can be neither a form of sponta-
neous social explosion nor a conspiratorial act; the proletariat revolution, for Marx, can only be a conscious social movement within
specific established relations of production. In other words, according to Marx, the proletariat revolution is not a form of self-action,
but it is a historically necessary action whose outcome is naturally
embedded in the institution of the civil society and more specifically in capitalism. Thus, in their book *The Holy Family, or Critique of
Critical Criticism* (1845), Marx and Engels stress that the organization of the proletariat (the "mass") reflects the organization of the
capitalist society. Marx repeated this argument in *The Communist
Manifesto* (1848), where he argues that the proletariat is "the most
authentic product" of the big industry. Additionally, in his *Revolution and Anti-Revolution in Germany* (1851), Marx argues that, due to
some historical necessity that is familiar to the communist 'hiero-
phants', a big, rich, concentrated and powerful bourgeoisie creates
a large, concentrated, powerful and intelligent proletarian class,
i.e., he believes that even the proletariat's spiritual qualities depend
on the situation of the bourgeoisie within the context of dialectic
materialism.

Even though Marx strives for the emancipation of man, he attempts to explain human history in terms of its conformity to universal rational laws, thus leaving the relationship between necessity and freedom ambiguous. Karl Kautsky, who, after the death

304 Karl Marx, *The Capital* (edited by F. Engels), New York: International
Publishers (originally published in 1894), Vol. III, Chapter 48.

of Engels, stood out as the most influential theorist of the Second International, emphasized the element of necessity in Marxism. Kautsky's conception of social evolution was always tied to that of natural evolution, and, thus, his analyses and critiques of capitalism are characterized by excessive emphasis on productive forces and objective necessity[305]. In general, the lack of explicit acknowledgment of the significance of the kairicity of human consciousness made many Marxist scholars susceptible to historical determinism and propheticism.

By ignoring the critical role of kairicity, several Marxist analyses of capitalism have failed to recognize that the crisis of the capitalist society is not a narrowly economic one, but it has to do with the extent to which and the manner in which social actors operate in accordance with the dialectic of kairicity. Consumerism and the bureaucratic form of social organization deprive many people of the ability to operate in a kairic manner and also of the awareness of the dialectic of kairicity. As I have already argued in this book, kairicity is the most important factor of production. On the other hand, consumerism and the bureaucratic form of social organization undermine kairicity, and in fact they tend to reduce kairicity to a minimal level, by cultivating linear, conformist ways of thinking and acting. Therefore, the ultimate and most decisive cause of the crisis of the capitalist society is not the unequal distribution of ownership but the alienation[306] of the human being that is caused by consumerism and by the bureaucratic form of social organization. For instance, in the Soviet Union, the abolition of private ownership of the factors of production did not solve the problems of exploitation and alienation; the Soviet worker was being exploited and alienated inside the Soviet factory due to the latter's bureaucratic organization and due to the rigid vertical mode of organization of the Soviet Union's communist party.

---

305 See: Leszek Kolakowski, *Main Currents of Marxism*, 3 vols, Oxford: Oxford University Press, 1978.

306 'Alienation' is associated with the removability or irremovability of property and of such immaterial possessions as liberties and rights and with the features that people are said to share by virtue of being citizens and/ or human beings.

The physiocratic fallacy in the context of socialism: In this case, the physiocratic fallacy consists in an attempt to apply a program of government intervention in the economy in order to help the market to achieve an equilibrium that is supposed to reflect the 'natural' state of affairs. The supporters of technocratic socialism[307] did not refute the core rationale of the physiocrats, but they proposed various models of 'mixed economy' simply because they thought that those models would be more successful in establishing and maintaining the 'natural' social-economic order. For instance, the French socialist Claude-Henri de Rouvroy Saint-Simon (1760–1825) has advocated the rational organization of industrial production under the direction of a skilled and trained elite. Moreover, the presentation of socialism as the rational use of economic resources led to the technocratic elitism of the Fabian Society and to various mathematically elegant but operationally problematic models of economic planning. For instance, the Polish economist Oskar Lange and the American economist Abba Lerner have proposed a model of market socialism were a central planning bureau would adjust prices of publicly-owned firms to equal marginal cost to enhance the market mechanism by achieving Pareto[308] efficient outcomes.

The physiocratic fallacy in the context of ecologism: In this case, the physiocratic fallacy consists in an attempt to explain the 'natural' social-economic order by giving primacy to biological-environmental factors. Furthermore, the ideological core of ecologism is poor. Freeden argues that the ideological core of ecologism consists of four concepts only — namely, the relationship between human beings and nature, valued preservation, holism and implementation of ecological lifestyles — and that these "are insufficient on their

---

307 For a methodical study of socialism, see: G.D.H. Cole, *A History of Socialist Thought*, 7 vols, London: Macmillan, 1953–1960; Albert Fried and Ronald Sanders (eds), *Socialist Thought: A Documentary History*, Edinburgh: Edinburgh University Press, 1964.

308 The term 'Pareto efficiency' (or 'allocative efficiency') refers to "a situation in which no reorganization of trade could raise the utility or satisfaction of one individual without lowering the utility or satisfaction of another individual. Under certain limited conditions, perfect competition leads to allocative efficiency"; Samuelson and Nordhaus, *Economics*, p. 729.

own to conjure up a vision or interpretation of human and social interaction and purposes"[309]. According to Freeden, the 'green core' of ecologism does not even "point...in a direction of a clear method of reacting to such visions and interpretations"[310]. Thus, within the framework of ecologism, "nature becomes an overriding factor in guiding human conduct"[311], and "the finiteness of resources"[312] and "the interdependence of all forms of life"[313] are stressed. Thus, from this standpoint, ecologism reduces to an attempt to add further constraints to the model of natural equilibrium that was originally formulated by the physiocrats. In other words, in the 20th century and in the beginning of the 21st century, the main representatives of ecologism do not refute the physiocratic core of neoclassical economics and its utilitarian ethos, but mainly they try to expand the set of constraints that neoclassical economists use in their 'constrained-optimization' models.

The physiocratic character of ecologism promotes an 'ecological Puritanism' (based on the promotion of 'clean'/ 'green' products and services). Like the Puritanism of the pioneers of the capitalist system, the Puritanism of ecologism is based on man's conformity to an assumed natural order of things that imposes its unquestionable necessities on the human being. Thus, like the Puritanism of the pioneers of capitalism, the Puritanism of ecologism gives rise to various new profit-seeking enterprises in the field of 'green economy', which preserve the core mentality and ethos of the 18th century founders of capitalism. For instance, on October 10, 2008, in an interview with Bill Moyers of PBS, the well-known financial speculator George Soros stated that the business of green could serve as the new "motor of the world economy".

To the extent that ecologism follows the physiocratic rationale and generally adopts the fundamental ontological and epistemological theses of classical and neoclassical economics, the kind of eco-

---

309 Michael Freeden, *Ideologies and Political Theory*, Oxford: Oxford University Press, 1996, p. 527.

310 Ibid., p. 527.

311 Ibid., p. 527.

312 Ibid., p. 527.

313 Ibid., p. 527.

logical responsibility that is promoted by the ideology of ecologism is derived from the thesis that the reality of nature consists in a set of necessities that are independent of human consciousness and to which human consciousness must succumb and conform and from the feeling that nature is an objective condition in which we live and to which we must adapt in the most efficient manner. Thus, ultimately, ecologism reduces social life to the determinism of 'natural choice'. On the other hand, from the standpoint of kairology, which I defend in this book, ecological responsibility is derived from the anthropocentric thesis that there is a dynamic continuity between the reality of the world (including the 'natural world') and the reality of consciousness and from the feeling that man is (or at least has to act as) the wise manager of nature. Therefore, from the standpoint of kairology, ecological responsibility is not merely a mode of behavior, but it is a mode of existence. In other words, if, as I argue in this book, the existence of the human being is characterized by the dynamic continuity between nature and consciousness and by the ability of human consciousness to restructure and utilize reality according to the dialectic of kairicity, then ecological responsibility is identified with kairicity, and, thus, it is an outcome of free choice and not a code of conduct dictated by natural determinism. The ecological responsibility of the human being should not be attributed to its nature, but it should be attributed to its mode of existence, i.e., to kairicity. In other words, human beings are and must be ecologically responsible beings not because they are *parts* of the natural world but because they are *kairic persons* and, more specifically, *kairic managers* of nature. Hence, due to the kairicity of human consciousness, far from undermining human autonomy, ecological responsibility proves to be an expression of human autonomy.

CHAPTER 18. THE DEMOCRATIC MICROSTRUCTURES AND MACROSTRUCTURES OF KAIROLOGICAL ECONOMICS

Several mainstream economists often try to defend their approach to economics not by answering the important philosophical questions that are interwoven with economic research but by arguing that all those who criticize classical and neoclassical economics are 'radicals' or 'leftists' and by boasting that the governments that won the game of the Cold War were intellectually guided by the classical and neoclassical economic thought. Apart from the fact that this kind of response to criticism is based on propaganda and not on scientific discourse and it ignores that, as I have shown in this book, the physiocratic fallacy pervades both the mainstream economic thought of the West and the mainstream economic thought of the 'Soviet Bloc', it also keeps the scientific discipline of economics intellectually anchored in obsolete ontological, epistemological and moral assumptions.

Paul Samuelson and William Nordhaus, following Assar Lindbeck's[314] review of 'radical economics', write that "the radicals mis-

314 Assar Lindbeck, *The Political Economy of the New Left: An Outsider's View*, New York: Harper & Row, 1971.

trust both the private market and the state bureaucracy", and they go on as follows: "that is one dislike too many, for these two systems are the only existing mechanisms by which a modern economy can allocate its resources"[315]. In contrast to the 'radical economics' that Assar Lindbeck, Paul Samuelson and William Nordhaus have in mind, the kairological theory of economics that I defend in this book includes a critique of theories of the private market and the state bureaucracy that is motivated not by mistrust toward the logical structures of those theories but by trust in the kairic operation of human consciousness. In other words, from the standpoint of kairology, the main problem of economic theory is not the discovery of economic laws and the creation of consistent grand logical structures to which economic actors must conform, but the methodical study of the kairic action of the human being and especially of the manner in which the autonomy of the human being is manifested in the economic field. Hence, kairological economics marks a shift in focus from economic theories that are (explicitly or implicitly) based on obsolete ontological, epistemological and moral theses to an economic theory that is based on the philosophical thesis that there is a dynamic continuity between the reality of the world and the reality of consciousness and on the kairicity of consciousness.

In the sequel, I analyze the democratic microstructures and macrostructures of kairological economics, and I argue that these democratic structures are morally superior to the standard structures of (neo)classical economics and simultaneously they are more efficient modes of social and economic organization than the standard structures of (neo)classical economics, because they are focused on the kairic action of the human being, and, therefore, they can account for the complexity and the indeterminacy of social life.

At the heart of the democratic microstructures of kairological economics lies the concept of kairological management. Kairological management is founded on the dialectic of kairicity, and, therefore, it is an important, substantial, feasible and efficient alternative to technocratic management. Both (neo)classical economics (i.e., the Western economic orthodoxy throughout the 20ᵗʰ century) and

---

315 Samuelson and Nordhaus, *Economics*, p. 382.

state capitalism (e.g. the economic model of the Soviet Union and Maoist China) are based on technocratic management, which, in Alvin Toffler's words, has the following defects:

> First, technocratic planning, itself a product of industrialism, reflects the values of that fast-vanishing era. In both its capitalist and communist variants, industrialism was a system focused on the maximization of material welfare...Technocratic planning is *econocentric*. Second, technocratic planning reflects the time-bias of industrialism. Struggling to free itself from the stifling past-orientation of previous societies, industrialism focused heavily on the present. This meant, in practice, that its planning dealt with futures near at hand...Technocratic planning is *short-range*. Third, reflecting the bureaucratic organization of industrialism, technocratic planning was premised on hierarchy...This system, adequate while change unfolds at an industrial tempo, breaks down as the pace reaches super industrial speeds. The increasingly unstable environment demands more and more non-programmed decisions down below; the need for instant feedback blurs the distinction between line and staff; and hierarchy totters...technocratic planning is essentially *undemocratic*.[316]

In addition, the so-called rationalization of capitalist production is in essence a set of contradictions, since it is based on the organization of work without the involvement of the workers, thus marginalizing the workers' human role and personhood, which is an absurdity even from the standpoint of economic efficiency.

Furthermore, bureaucratization has meant that the fundamental social relationship of technocratic capitalist systems, i.e., the relationship between directors and executants, gradually weakens the ability of big portions of society to think and act according to the dialectic of kairicity, because it diffuses conformism, promotes moral abdication and undermines the intellectual progress of humanity. In other words, bureaucratization has meant that technocratic capitalist structures deprive more and more people of the ability to think and act creatively and of the ability to take personal responsibilities for their professional and personal life. Thus, big portions of society gradually lapse into a state of uncontrolled emotionalism that reduces civic freedom to consumerism and to a self-destructive social ethic promoted by the 'entertainment indus-

---

316 Alvin Toffler, *Future Shock*, New York: Bantam Books, 1971, pp. 448-449.

try' and divorces civic freedom from civic responsibility. We should never ignore that, as Stephen Davies has argued, "a social order in which responsibility is denied and rights limited will erode virtuous behavior until it is faced with a stark choice between moral chaos and the attempt to enforce virtue by force".[317]

From the 1960s onwards, in Europe and North America, the labor class's attitude toward bureaucratic organizations shows that they see them as alien institutions. Less and less members of the labor class still believe that 'their' parties or trade unions are willing or able to bring about a major change in their situation. They may express various types of support to bureaucratic organizations but they only treat them as a lesser evil and only use them as one uses a lawyer, a policeman, or a food seller. They rarely mobilize themselves for them and do not actively participate in them. Thus, political parties rely more and more on paid staff and comply more and more with the norms of the 'entertainment industry'.

The democratization of the social organization presupposes a high degree of social and political consciousness among the entire society. It can be neither the result of a mere revolt against exploitation nor the outcome of elections themselves, but it can arise only from the capacity of the entire society to extract from itself positive answers to the problems involved in the reconstruction of modern society and from the capacity of the entire society to act according to the dialectic of kairicity. No individual, group or party can be delegated this consciousness and kairicity 'on behalf of' society or in its stead. A substitution of this sort would inevitably lead to the formation of a new group of rulers and would preserve the alienation of the working class.[318] Furthermore, it is impossible for a particular group to take on such tasks, because these tasks are so big and so complex that can be dealt with only by society as a whole. Alvin Toffler has stressed that the crisis of modern regimes is a con-

---

317 Stephen Davies, "Towards the Remoralization of Society", in M. Loney et al. (eds), *The State or the Market*, London: Sage, 1987, p. 174.
318 The tragic degradation of the socialist movement in the Soviet Union and the transformation of the Western democratic movement into a form of liberal oligarchy are characteristic examples of these phenomena.

sequence of the fact that the direction of society is a task that, at least in the era of advanced modernity or 'super-industrial society', is beyond the capacity of any particular category:

> Democratic political forms arose in the West...because the historical pressure toward social differentiation and toward faster paced systems demanded sensitive social feedback. In complex, differentiated societies, vast amounts of information must flow at ever faster speeds between the formal organizations and subcultures that make up the whole, and between the layers and sub-structures within these. Political democracy, by incorporating larger and larger numbers in social decision-making, facilitates feedback. And it is precisely this feedback that is essential to control...The technocrat, however, still thinking in top-down terms, frequently makes plans without arranging for adequate and instantaneous feedback from the field, so that he seldom knows how well are working. When he does arrange for feedback, what he usually asks for and gets is heavily economic, inadequately social, psychological or cultural. Worse yet, he makes these plans without sufficiently taking into account the fast-changing needs and wishes of those whose participation is needed to make them a success.[319]

The problem of the creation of a consciously kairic social and economic organization cannot be solved or even be correctly posed without the deployment of the kairic activity of the immense majority of the members of the given social-economic organization. For, the real meaning of this reconstruction is that everything must be reexamined and refashioned: markets, modes and relations of production, consumption, ideas, educational systems, political institutions and science itself — according to the kairicity of the consciousness of the immense majority of the members of the given social-economic organization. The previous reconstruction is significant because of the following reasons: (i) It marks an anthropocentric reorganization of the social-economic system. (ii) It generates understanding by clarifying values and arguments in policy debates. (iii) It reduces complexity and generates insights through research and analysis. (iv) It helps safeguard against uncertainty. (v) It creates consensus by involving stakeholders in policy process.

> Thus, a new kind of information system is necessary: a loop rather than a ladder. Information must pulse through this loop at accelerating speeds, with the output of one group becoming

---

319 Toffler, *Future Shock*, pp. 475-476.

the input for many others, so that no group, however politically potent it may seem, can independently set goals for the whole.[320]

Democratic microstructures

The democratic microstructures of kairological economics consist in organizations that are based on kairological management and on the workers' participation in the management. Kairological management is a form of management that aims at making an organization operate in a kairic state, where negative feedback coexists with positive feedback, and stability coexists with instability, as I explained in Chapter 3. Kairological management leads to the realization of the organizational vision of the management consultant Bernard Muller-Thym, who has said:

> What is now within our grasp is a kind of productive capability that is alive with intelligence, alive with information, so that at its maximum it is completely flexible; one could completely reorganize the plant from hour to hour if one wished to do so.[321]

Additionally, the democratic microstructures of kairological economics are based on the radical modification of bureaucratic hierarchies. This can be achieved by a radical modification of corporate law and labor law. The four defining characteristics of the modern corporation[322] are: (i) separate legal personality of the corporation; (ii) shares; (iii) limited liability of the shareholders; (iv) delegated management (i.e., control of the company placed in the hands of a board of directors). A kairological reformation of traditional corporate law must bring about the following change: in every corporation, a portion (e.g. the two-thirds) of the members of the board of directors must be elected by the annual general assembly of the company's shareholders and another portion (e.g. the one-third) of the members of the board of directors must be elected by the annual general assembly of the given company's employees. Moreover, in the context of such a kairological corporate law, each board of directors must be free to form and reform its by-laws by

---

320 Ibid., p. 476.
321 Quoted in: Toffler, *Future Shock*, p. 136.
322 See: R.C. Clark, *Corporate Law*, New York: Aspen Publishers, 1986.

making decisions according to the majority rule and, of course, in compliance with the established public and private law. In other words, each member of the board of directors that has been elected by the annual general assembly of the company's shareholders and each member of the board of directors that has been elected by the annual general assembly of the company's employees have one vote, and all these members together form and reform the by-laws that regulate the details of the operation of the board of directors by se-lecting alternatives which have a majority, i.e., more than half the votes.

Under the previous kairological corporate law, both the capital-ist class and the labor class have to become more responsible and more sophisticated in their judgments and actions, are obliged to develop a more alert consciousness, and also they become increas-ingly aware that, in essence, business decision-making is a grand training experience in kairological economics. More specifically, the main objectives of the previous kairic amendment of corporate law are the following: (i) A kairic reorganization of the relationship between capitalists and workers and more generally between direc-tors and executants. (ii) An instrument for increasing efficiency of enterprises and promoting behaviors that are in accordance with the dialectic of kairicity. (iii) A device for developing kairological education and promoting the morality of personal responsibility. (iv) An institutional way of developing personal and social au-tonomy. (v) A means for creating more efficient feedback systems, which lead to higher productivity and increased production.

Democratic macrostructures

The democratic macrostructures of kairological economics consist in political institutions that secure personal and social au-tonomy. Social autonomy means the participation of the citizen in state processes, or, in other words, the citizen's control over state actions. Personal autonomy means the protection of the citizen against invasion of his private sphere of life and human and civil rights by the state and by other citizens, and also it means the abil-ity and the right of the individual to create norms for itself. The principles of social autonomy, personal autonomy and the separation of powers are explicitly emphasized by the 1776 U.S. Declaration of Independence and by the U.S. Constitution. In fact, as the preamble to the U.S. Constitution acknowledges, the American people established government in order to "spread the blessings of liberty" to themselves and to their posterity. Thus, Joseph William Singer, Professor of Law at Harvard Law School, has argued that "the task of progressives is to articulate a philosophy of humanity and democracy that will enable us to reimagine and revitalize basic American values of liberty, equality and property while making the free market work for everyone"[323].

The first goal of the democratic macrostructures of kairological economics is to impose restrictions on the concentration of state authority. This can be achieved through the regional decentralization of the processes through which social decisions are made. The higher the level of regional decentralization is the more effective the attempt of forging social autonomy becomes. Hayek[324] has discussed the use of knowledge in society, emphasizing that local governments have better access to local information, and, therefore, they can provide public goods and services that better match local preferences than the national government. Tiebout[325] has introduced the inter-jurisdictional competition dimension and has argued that such a competition provides a decision-making mechanism to better match public goods and services with consumers' preferences. Based on these ideas, Musgrave[326] and Oates[327] have created a theory of fiscal federalism, emphasizing the appropriate

---

323 J.W. Singer, "Democratic Values and the American Constitution Society", *Harvard Law and Policy Review Online*, September 18, 2006.

324 F.A. Hayek, "The Use of Knowledge in Society", *American Economic Review*, Vol. 35, 1945, pp. 519-530.

325 Charles Tiebout, "A Pure Theory of Local Expenditures", *Journal of Political Economy*, Vol. 64, 1956, pp. 416-424.

326 Richard Musgrave, *Theory of Public Finance: A Study in Public Economy*, New York: McGraw-Hill, 1959.

327 Wallace Oates, *Fiscal Federalism*, New York: Harcourt Brace Jovanovich, 1972.

assignment of taxes and expenditures to the various levels of government to improve welfare.

The second goal of the democratic macrostructures of kairological economics is the fairness of political competition. All political parties and social movements must have equal and free access to the media, without any discrimination. Special laws must secure that the media (TV channels, radio channels, newspapers, etc.) treat all political parties and all social movements in a fair manner.

Moreover, it should be emphasized that the workers' participation in the management, according to the kairic reformation of corporate law and labor law that I proposed above, is a decisive and necessary step toward the democratization of the media. Robert McChesney has argued that the case for media democratization is based on the following two propositions:

> First, *media perform essential political, social, economic, and cultural functions in modern democracies...*Democracy requires a media system that provides people with a wide range of opinion and analysis and debate on important issues, reflects the diversity of citizens, and promotes public accountability of the powers-that-be and the powers-that-want-to-be...Second, *media organization — patterns of ownership, management, regulation, and subsidy — is a central determinant of media content.*[328]

Given that corporate ownership and commercial pressures influence media content, decisively affecting the range of news, opinions, and entertainment citizens receive, the principle of the workers' participation in the management leads to a more democratic, more transparent and more efficient system of media management, which, in turn, leads to a more equal and more efficient distribution of economic, social, cultural, and information capital, thus giving rise to a more enlightened representative political discourse.

The third goal of the democratic macrostructures of kairological economics is the promotion of transparency in political decision-making. This can be achieved through the workers' participation in the management of corporations, through the control of political parties by the citizens who are members of them, and through the

---

328 R.W. McChesney, "Making Media Democratic", *Boston Review*, Vol. 23, 1998, pp. 4–10, 20.

public disclosure of the processes through which major political decisions are made at all levels of government.

The fourth goal of the democratic macrostructures of kairological economics is the democratization and humanization of the welfare state. The classical conception of the welfare state understands the system of social security simply as a means of reforming the negative consequences of a morally neutral and ruthless techno-economic system. Thus, in the context of the classical conception of the welfare state, the social security system is associated with bureaucratic oppression, statism and inefficiency[329], and control is elusive. In fact, Lipsky has argued that the work of street-level bureaucrats occurs at a remove of direct oversight and additionally it involves a core of irreducible discretion[330]. On the other hand, from the standpoint of kairological economics, the welfare state should signify the domination of the human being on labor and the destruction of the bureaucratic mythology, according to which what people themselves do and know is a private little matter of their own that does not really matter while really important matters are the monopoly of those who occupy the apex of the socio-economic pyramid, i.e., a new priesthood of big capital owners and experts in various endeavors.

From the standpoint of kairological economics, the administration of the social security system should be directly accountable to the workers. This can be achieved by merging all social security funds into a single national social security fund (NSSF). Every public and private sector employee should be obliged to have a NSSF

---

329 For instance, J. Fried has argued that "since 1935, the mechanisms used by Social Security to transfer wealth have become simplistic and counterproductive — made obsolete by the enormous changes in individual finance and family structure...Almost no one gets his 'individual direct contributions invested at interest'. In fact, many get no interest at all, and lose much of what they contributed...When it comes time to divvy up the benefits, there are some winners and many losers in the Social Security system"; see: Joseph Fried, *How Social Security Picks Your Pocket — A Story of Waste, Fraud, and Inequities*, New York: Algora Publishing, 2003, p. 27.

330 Michael Lipsky, *Street-Level Bureaucracy: The Dilemmas of Individuals in Public Services*, New York: Russell Sage Foundation, 1980.

account. Additionally, every public and private sector employee should be obliged to contribute 5% of his monthly wages to his NSSF account, and his employer (whether the state or a non-state employer) should be obliged to contribute another 5% of the given employee's monthly wages to the given employee's NSSF account for the sake of the given employee[331]. There should be no other financial contributions to the NSSF on behalf of the government, and the contributions of the employees and the employers to the NSSF should be fully tax deductible. Self-employed workers should be allowed to enter the NSSF system, if they wished, thus creating an incentive for informal workers to join the formal economy. The management of the NSSF should be in the hands of a board of directors that should be composed as follows: the one half of the members of this board of directors should be elected by the annual assembly of all the employees who have a NSSF account (including those self-employed workers who have a NSSF account); the one fourth of the members of this board of directors should be appointed by the government on an annual basis; and the other one fourth of the members of this board of directors should be elected by the annual assembly of all the private sector employers who make financial contributions to the NSSF for the sake of their employees. The NSSF should be subject to government regulation intended to guarantee a diversified and low-risk portfolio and to prevent theft or fraud, and the Central Bank should provide oversight. Furthermore, private insurance companies should continue to operate offering their own life insurance and medical care programs. Finally,

---

331 The management of the transition to the NSSF system should make provisions for those who would already receive a pension according to the old system and for those who would already contribute to the old system. In particular, the government should guarantee those already receiving a pension that their pensions would be unaffected by the reform, and it should give a 'recognition bond' to every worker who leaves the old system and moves to the new NSSF system (this 'recognition bond' would represent the contributions of each worker to the old system and should be deposited to the corresponding worker's NSSF account).

the government could apply a system of negative income tax[332] to help the poor and the handicapped to achieve an above subsistence living. In other words, the negative income tax system is designed to alleviate unavoidable needs.

The fifth goal of the democratic macrostructures of kairological economics is the democratization of the banking-credit system. Peter Bond has summarized and explained the system of financial intermediation as follows:

> In any economy there will be at any given time two groups of economic agents: (i) those we term *SURPLUS UNITS*, i.e., those whose revenue exceeds their current expenditure during the period under consideration...(ii) those we term *DEFICIT UNITS*, i.e., those whose expenditure exceeds their current revenue in a given time period. Given the existence of surplus units and deficit units, some mechanism is required to ensure that the surplus funds are channeled to the deficit units...it is very often the case that the individual with surplus funds will lend them to a financial institution or *financial intermediary* which will then on-lend these funds by itself buying company shares, government stocks or whatever assets it normally invests in.[333]

Additionally, Peter Bond has explained the role of banks as follows:

> Amongst the many types of financial intermediary, the banks have a special place because they are the prime providers of money in a modern economy...One common feature of all banks is *the taking of deposits*...A second common feature is that of *the encashment of deposits*...The third (and in many ways the most distinctive) feature of banks is the transfer of deposits to third parties, for the most part by way of cheques but also via standing orders, direct debits and other transfer mechanisms.[334]

Gradually, during the 20th century and the beginning of the 21st century, through the development of financial engineering, through the accumulation of power and capital, and through globalization,

---

332 The idea of negative income tax is commonly thought to have originated with economist Milton Friedman, who advocated it in his 1962 book, *Capitalism and Freedom*. However, Joseph Pechman, long-time tax dean of the Brookings Institution, has credited the University of Wisconsin's Robert Lampman with at least simultaneous formulation of the concept of negative income tax.

333 Peter Bond, *Monetary Economics*, Worcester: Northwick Publishers, 1989, p. 24.

334 Ibid., p. 28.

banks (as well as other financial intermediaries) created a financial system whose operation becomes more and more disengaged from and independent of the reality of the productive forces of the economy — namely, from the economic sectors of agriculture, industry and services — and the needs of the people. In this context, the asset function of money acquires increasing importance versus the exchange function of money, and the trade of money tends to become an end in itself and a means by which the banking system tends to dominate the entire economic system, instead of operating as a servant of the productive forces of the economy. Thus, for instance, at the dawn of 2010, the banks and credit institutions that created the financial crisis due to their arrogance and greed and due to their overconfidence in complex models of financial engineering, engaged the governments in the dilemma of 'either you save us (i.e., banks) or you will incur destructive consequences as governments and as economies'. Governments used taxpayers' money in order to offer enormous financial support to the banking system, helping the bankers to win the battle against bankruptcy. However, the financial crisis, which was caused by the banks, became the cause of bankruptcy for many people and firms in various economic fields, and the banks — even though they were saved by the taxpayers' money, and not by the supposed skills of their highly-paid managers — were reluctant to lend money to firms that were trying to survive and develop in the middle of a financial crisis and to people who were trying to satisfy rational needs and wishes. The financial crisis that broke out in 2010 is a dramatic example of the consequences of an inefficient and undemocratic banking system.

In order to build an efficient and democratic banking system, banks must be directly placed under the control and in the service of the productive forces of the economy and society at large. This can be achieved through a major reformation of the banking system. In particular, the only legitimate form of commercial banks must be that of a credit cooperative[335]. In other words, all commercial banks

---

335 For instance, in 2003, the European Union started facilitating cooperatives through Council Regulation No. 1435/ 2003 of July 22, 2003 on the Statute for a European Cooperative Society.

must become credit cooperatives. A credit cooperative is a financial intermediary that aims for the economic, social, entrepreneurial, housing, environmental and cultural development of its members. Normally, only a member of a credit cooperative may deposit money with the credit cooperative or borrow money from it, and, thus, the members who have accounts in the credit cooperative are the owners of the credit cooperative and they elect their board of directors in a democratic one-person-one-vote system. Moreover, a credit cooperative can accept investors, in the form of either physical or legal entities, as members who will have no intention to use or produce the given credit cooperative's goods and services, but who wish to invest their capital and simultaneously support the given credit cooperative.

Each member of a credit cooperative is liable up to the nominal value of his shares, and he is registered for one mandatory cooperative share. He can, however, acquire more optional cooperative shares, according to the relevant law. All cooperative shares are registered, and both mandatory and optional shares are of equal value and produce the same rights and obligations with the exception of the members' voting rights. Each member participates in the shareholders' general assembly with one vote, regardless of the number of cooperative shares that he may own. The cooperative share is not liable to seizure for debts of a cooperative member to third parties, nor assigned or licensed in any way for insurance or guarantee to a third party for any reason or purpose.

A credit cooperative's funds consist of cooperative shares, the legal reserves that are determined by the Central Bank, the extra reserves, the special reserves, any tax-free reserves, the earnings from the cooperative shares (over par value), all kinds of donations, grants, subsidies, etc., as well as assets eligible for valuation by an expert appointed according to the established legal system, and other contributions to be determined by the board of directors. Moreover, a credit cooperative can raise additional funds through special participations of its members, through loans, through bonds, through special-purpose capital raisings (e.g. mutual funds, energy funds, real-estate funds, etc.).

By being members of credit cooperatives, physical and legal entities can create a banking system that directly reflects their interests and serves their needs and goals. Thus, through the system of credit cooperatives, society and especially the productive forces of the economy exert active democratic control over the monetary subsystem of the economy. For instance, federations of industries, trade unions, agricultural cooperatives, municipalities, professional associations, chambers, and other legal entities can create credit cooperatives, which will be firmly oriented toward the prosperity of the credit cooperatives' members. Moreover, by becoming members of credit cooperatives, young scientists, young self-employed professionals and young small companies can find financial support for good ideas that they may have about the development of their activities and projects.

From the standpoint of kairology, which I advocate in this book, the determining characteristic of history is the creativity of the human being. Furthermore, from the standpoint of kairology, a society is really democratic only when it is aware that, due to the kairicity of human consciousness, it is the given society that creates its institutions. Hence, the primary question in political economy is the methodical and systematic inquiry into the kairicity of the human consciousness in the field of political economy, and not the formulation and application of economic laws that are assumed to be independent of human consciousness.

In the context of kairological economics, the purpose of the economic system is to cultivate and promote the kairic action of the human being and of groups of human beings in their political-economic relations and actions, and the purpose of economic theory is to study the kairicity of the human being and of groups of human beings in their political-economic relations and actions. From the standpoint of kairological economics, the future is not given, and, therefore, every question about the exact form of the future that will emerge from the kairic action of man is cognitively insignificant. The kairological management of political and economic affairs is founded on discretion and alert consciousness.

Bibliography

Alpert, M. and Raiffa, H., "A Progress Report on the Training of Probability Assessors", in D. Kahneman, P. Slovic and A. Tversky (eds), *Judgment Under Uncertainty: Heuristics and Biases*, Cambridge: Cambridge University Press, 1982

Anderla, G., Anthony Dunning and Simon Forge, *Chaotics*, Twickenham: Adamantine Press, 1997

Anteby, M., *Moral Gray Zones*, Princeton: Princeton University Press, 2008

Argyris, C., *Overcoming Organizational Defenses: Facilitating Organizational Learning*, Boston: Allen & Bacon, Prentice-Hall, 1990

Armor, D.A. and Taylor, S.E.(eds), "When Predictions Fail: The Dilemma of Unrealistic Optimism", in T. Gilovich, D. Griffin and D. Kahneman (eds), *Heuristics and Biases: The Psychology of Intuitive Judgment*, Cambridge: Cambridge University Press, 2002

Aune, B., *Kant's Theory of Morals*, Princeton, NJ: Princeton University Press, 1979

Axelrod, R., *The Evolution of Cooperation*, New York: Basic Books, 1984

Barberis, N., Shleifer, A. and Vishny, R., "A Model of Investor Sentiment", *Journal of Financial Economics*, Vol. 49, 1998

Barnard, C., *The Functions of the Executive*, Cambridge, MA: Harvard University Press, 1938

Barry, B. and Hardin, R. (eds), *Rational Man and Irrational Society? – An Introduction and Sourcebook*, Beverly Hills, Calif.: Sage, 1982

Beck, U., *Risk Society: Towards a New Modernity*, London: Sage, 1992

Bell, D., *The Coming of Post-Industrial Society*, New York: Basic Books, 1973

Belton, V., "Multiple Criteria Decision Analysis: Practically the Only Way to Choose", in L.C. Hendry and R.W. Engelese (eds), *OR Tutorial Papers*, Birmingham: Operational Research Society, 1990

Bendell, J., "Civil Regulation: A New Form of Democratic Governance for the Global Economy?", in J. Bendell (ed.), *Terms of Endearment: Business, NGOs and Sustainable Development*, Sheffield: Greenleaf Publishing, 2000

Bennett, P., Tait, A. and Macdonagh, K., "INTERACT: Developing Software for Interactive Decisions", *Group Decision and Negotiation*, Vol. 3, 1994

Bennett, P.G. and Dando, M.R., "Complex Strategic Analysis: A Study of the Fall of France", *Journal of Operational Research Society*, Vol. 33, 1979

Bentham, J., *An Introduction to the Principles of Morals and Legislation*, ed. J.H. Burns and H.L.A. Hart, London: Athlone Press, 1970 (originally published in 1789)

Bhaskar, R., *A Realist Theory of Science*, Brighton: Harvester, 1978

Black, B., *Anarchy after Leftism*, Columbia, MO: C.A.L. Press, 1997

Black, B., *Nightmares of Reason*, http://www.theanarchistlibrary.org

Black, F., "An Equilibrium Model of the Crash", *NBER Macroeconomics Annual* 1988, Vol. 3, National Bureau of Economic Research, Inc.

Bond, P., *Monetary Economics*, Worcester: Northwick Publishers, 1989

Boyd, R. and Richerson, P.J., "Cultural Transmission and the Evolution of Cooperative Behavior", *Human Ecology*, Vol. 10, 1982

Bragd, A. et al., "Beyond Greening: New Dialogue and New Approaches for Developing Sustainability", *Business Strategy and the Environment*, Vol. 7, 1998

Brim, O.G. et al., *Personality and Decision Processes: Studies in the Social Psychology of Thinking*, Stanford: Stanford University Press, 1962

Britton, K., *John Stuart Mill*, Harmondsworth: Penguin, 1953

Bronowski, J., *The Ascent of Man*, Boston: Little, 1974

Brown, D.P. and Jennings, R.H., "On Technical Analysis", *The Review of Financial Studies*, Vol. 2, 1989

Burton, J., *Resolving Deep-Rooted Conflicts*, Lanham: University Press of America, 1987

Busse, J.A. and Green, T.C., "Market Efficiency in Real Time", *Journal of Financial Economics*, Vol. 65, 2002

Bussmann, H., *Routledge Dictionary of Language and Linguistics*, London: Routledge, 1996

Cairnes, J.E., *The Character and Logical Method of Political Economy*, London: Macmillan, 1888

Calabresi, G., "Transaction Costs, Resource Allocation and Liability Rules: A Comment", *Journal of Law and Economics*, Vol. 11, 1968

Campbell, J., *Reference and Consciousness*, Oxford: Clarendon Press, 2002

Cassirer, E., *The Philosophy of Symbolic Forms*, Volume One: Language, Volume Two: Mythical Thought, trans. R. Manheim, New Haven: Yale University Press, 1955

Castells, M., *The Information Age: Economy, Society and Culture*, Oxford: Blackwell, 1997

Castoriadis, C., *The Imaginary Institution of Society*, London: Polity Press, 1987 (originally published in 1975 by Éditions du Seuil)

Clark, A.W., "The Effects of Unemployment on Political Attitude", *Journal of Sociology*, Vol. 21, 1985

Clark, R.C., *Corporate Law*, New York: Aspen Publishers, 1986

Coase, R., "The Nature of the Firm", *Economica*, Vol. 4, 1937

Coase, R., "The Problem of Social Cost", *Journal of Law and Economics*, Vol. 3, 1960

Coate, R.A. and Rosati, J.A., "Preface", in R.A. Coate and J.A. Rosati (eds), *The Power of Human Needs in World Society*, Boulder, Colorado: Lynn Rienner, 1988

Cole, G.D.H., *A History of Socialist Thought*, 7 vols, London: Macmillan, 1953-1960

Colman, J., *John Locke's Moral Philosophy*, Edinburgh: Edinburgh University Press, 1983

Commons, J.R., *Legal Foundations of Capitalism*, with a new introduction by J.E. Biddle and W.J. Samuels, New Jersey: Transaction Publishers, 2007 (originally published in 1924)

Cox, R., "Structural Issues of Global Governance: Implications for Europe", in S. Gill (ed.), *Gramsci, Historical Materialism and International Relations*, Cambridge: Cambridge University Press, 1993

Crisp, R., *Mill on Utilitarianism*, London: Routledge, 1997

Curd, M. and Cover, J.A., *Philosophy of Science: The Central Issues*, New York: W.W. Norton & Co., 1998

Dantzig, G.B., *Linear Programming and Extensions*, Princeton, NJ: Princeton University Press, 1963

Davies, s., "Towards the Remoralization of Society", in M. Loney et al. (eds), *The State or the Market*, London: Sage, 1987

Deichsel, S., "Against the Pragmatic Justification for realism in Economic Methodology", *Erasmus Journal for Philosophy and Economics*, Vol. 4, 2011

Denison, E.F., *Multifactor Productivity Measures*, 1988 and 1989, U.S. Department of Labor, March 1991

Denison, E.F., *Trends in American Economic Growth*, 1929-1982, Washington, DC: Brookings, 1985

Derrida, J., *Of Grammatology*, trans. and ed. G. Spivak, Baltimore, MD: Johns Hopkins University Press, 1976

Dewey, J., *How We Think*, in *Middle Works*, Vol. 6, 1978 (originally published in 1910)

Dreyfus, H.L. and Dreyfus, S.E., *Mind Over Machine: The Power of Human Intuition and Expertise in the Age of the Computer*, Oxford: Basil Blackwell, 1986

Dreyfus, H.L., "Intelligence Without Representation: Merleau-Ponty's Critique of Mental Representation", *Phenomenology and the Cognitive Sciences*, Vol. 1, 2002

Dreyfus, H.L., *What Computers Still Can't Do*, Cambridge, MA: M.I.T. Press, 1992

Edwards, W., "Conservatism in Human Information Processing", in B. Kleinmutz (ed.), *Formal Representation of Human Judgment*, New York: John Wiley and Sons, 1968

Ein-Dor, P. (ed.), *Artificial Intelligence in Economics and Management*, Dordrecht: Kluwer Academic Publishers, 1996

Elster, J. and Moene, K.O.(eds), *Alternatives to Capitalism*, Cambridge: Cambridge University Press, 1989

Elster, J., "Some Unresolved Problems in the Theory of Rational Behaviour", *Acta Sociologica*, Vol. 36, 1993

Elster, J., "The Market and the Forum: Three Varieties of Political Theory", in J. Elster and A. Hyland (eds), *Foundations of Social Choice Theory*, Cambridge: Cambridge University Press, 1986

Elster, J., *Explaining Social Behavior: More Nuts and Bolts for the Social Sciences*, Cambridge: Cambridge University Press, 2007

Elster, J., *Local Justice*, New York: Russeell Sage Foundation, 1992

Elster, J., *Making Sense of Marx*, Cambridge: Cambridge University Press, 1985

Elster, J., *Nuts and Bolts for the Social Sciences*, Cambridge: Cambridge University Press, 1989

Elster, J., *Ulysses and the Sirens: Studies in Rationality and Irrationality*, Cambridge: Cambridge University Press, 1979

Fama, E., "Efficient Capital Markets: A Review of Theory and Empirical Work", *Journal of Finance*, Vol. 25, 1970

Fama, E., "Perspectives on October 1987, Or What Did We Learn from the Crash?", in R.W. Kamphuis, Jr, R.C. Kormendi and J.W. Henry Watson (eds), *Black Monday and the Future of the Financial Markets*, Homewood, Ill.: Irwin, 1989

Feather, N.T., *The psychological Impact of Unemployment*, New York: Springer-Verlag, 1990

Feldstein, M., *The Economist*, June 13, 1992.

Fischhoff, B., Slovic, P. and Lichtenstein, S., "Knowing with Certainty: The Appropriateness of Extreme Confidence", *Journal of Experimental Psychology*, Vol. 3, 1977

Floridi, L., "Information", in L. Floridi (ed.), *The Blackwell Guide to the Philosophy of Computing and Information*, Oxford: Blackwell, 2003

Flynn, T., *Existentialism: A Very Short Introduction*, Oxford: Oxford University Press, 2006

Foucault, M., "Nietzsche, Genealogy, History", in P. Rabinow (ed.), *The Foucault Reader*, Harmondsworth, Peregrine Books, 1986

Foucault, M., *Language, Counter-Memory, Practice*, ed. D.F. Bouchard, Ithaca, NY: Cornell University Press, 1977

Fox, C.R. and Tversky, A.N., "Ambiguity Aversion and Comparative Ignorance", *Quarterly Journal of Economics*, Vol. 110, 1995

Fratzscher, M., "On Currency Crises and Contagion", European Central Bank, Working Paper Series 139, April 2002

Freeden, M., *Ideologies and Political Theory*, Oxford: Oxford University Press, 1996

Freeman, R.E., *Strategic Management: A Stakeholder Approach*, Boston: Pitman, 1984

Frenkel, J.A. and Mussa, M.L., "Monetary and Fiscal Policies in an Open Economy", *American Economic Review*, Vol. 71, 1981

Frey, B., *Happiness: A Revolution in Economics*, Cambridge, MA: The M.I.T. Press, 2008

Fried, A. and Sanders, R.(eds), *Socialist Thought: A Documentary History*, Edinburgh: Edinburgh University Press, 1964

Fried, J., *How Social Security Picks Your Pocket – A Story of Waste, Fraud, and Inequities*, New York: Algora Publishing, 2003

Friedman, M.(ed.), *Studies in the Quantity Theory of Money*, Chicago: University of Chicago Press, 1956

Friedman, M., *Essays in Positive Economics*, Chicago: University of Chicago Press, 1953

Fryer, D. and Ullah, P. (eds), *Unemployed People: Social and Psychological Perspectives*, Milton Keynes: Open University Press, 1987

Gadamer, H.-G., *Truth and Method*, London: Sheed and Ward, 1975

Galbraith, J.K., *American Capitalism*, Boston: Houghton Mifflin, 1952

George, E., Speech, January 31, 1995: http://www.brugesgroup.com

Godelier, M., *The Enigma of the Gift*, Chicago: University of Chicago Press, 1999

Gordon, H., *Dictionary of Existentialism*, New York: Greenwood Press, 1999

Guyer, P.(ed.), *Kant's Groundwork of the Metaphysics of Morals: Critical Essays*, Lantham, MD: Rowman and Littlefield, 1998

Habermas, J., *Knowledge and Human Interests*, Cambridge: Polity, 1987 (first published 1968)

Habermas, J., *The Theory of Communicative Action, Vol. 2: The Critique of Functionalist Reason*, Cambridge: Polity, 1987

Hakim, C., "The Social Consequences of High Unemployment", *Journal of Social Policy*, Vol. 11, 1982

Hamilton, W.H., "The Institutional Approach to Economic Theory", *American Economic Review*, Vol. 9, 1919

Hampden-Turner, C., *Charting the Corporate Mind*, New York: Free Press/ Macmillan, 1990

Hands, D.W., *Testing, Rationality, and Progress: Essays on the Popperian Tradition in Economic Methodology*, Lanham, MD: Rowman & Littlefield Publishers, 1992

Harré, R., *Varieties of Realism*, Oxford: Blackwell, 1986

Hart, H.L.A., *Law, Liberty, and Morality*, Stanford: Stanford University Press, 1963

Hausman, D., *The Inexact and Separate Science of Economics*, Cambridge: Cambridge University Press, 1992

Hayek, F.A., "The Use of Knowledge in Society", *American Economic Review*, Vol. 35, 1945

Held, D., *Introduction to Critical Theory*, Berkeley, CA: University of California Press, 1980

Hempel, C.G., *Aspects of Concept Formation in Empirical Science*, Chicago: University of Chicago Press, 1965

Henkel, H., *Introduction to the Philosophy of Right*, trans. G.E. Ordeig, Madrid: Taurus, 1968

Higgins, B., "Elements of Indeterminacy in the Theory of Non-Perfect Competition", *American Economic Review*, Vol. 29, 1939

Hobsbawm, E., *The Age of Revolution*, London: Pelican, 1962

Hodgson, G.M., "Dichotomizing the Dichotomy: Veblen versus Ayres", in S. Fayazmanesh and M.R. Tool (eds), *Institutionalist Method and Value: Essays in Honour of Paul Dale Bush*, Cheltenham: Edward Elgar, 1998, Vol. I

Hoffman, E. and Spitzer, M.L., "The Coase Theorem: Some Experimental Tests", *Journal of Law and Economics*, Vol. 25, 1982

Hollis, M. and Lukes, S. (eds), *Rationality and Relativism*, Cambridge, Mass.: MIT Press, 1979

Hollis, M., "Why Elster is Stuck and Needs to Recover His Faith", *London Review of Books*, January 13, 1991

Hunt, L. et al., *The Challenge of the West*, Lexington, MA: D.C. Health & Company, 1995

Jahoda, M., *Employment and Unemployment: A Social-Psychological Analysis*, Cambridge: Cambridge University Press, 1982

Johansson, I., *A Critique of Karl Popper's Methodology*, Stockholm: Scandinavian University Books, 1975

Kahneman, D. and Tversky, A. (eds), *Choices, Values and Frames*, Cambridge: Cambridge University Press, 2000

Kahneman, D., Slovic, P. and Tversky, A. (eds), *Judgment Under Uncertainty: Heuristics and Biases*, Cambridge: Cambridge University Press, 1982

Kaminsky, G., Lizondo, S. and Reinhardt, C., "Leading Indicators of Currency Crises", International Monetary Fund, Western Hemisphere Department, Working Paper No. WP/97/79, July 1997

Kauffman, S.A., "Antichaos and Adaptation", *Scientific American*, August 1991

Kauffman, S.A., *Origins of Order: Self-organization and Selection in Evolution*, Oxford: Oxford University Press, 1993

Keynes, J.M., *The General Theory of Employment, Interest and Money*, London: Macmillan, 2007 (originally published in 1936)

Kincaid, H., *Philosophical Foundations of the Social Sciences: Analyzing Controversies in Social Research*, Cambridge: Cambridge University Press, 1996

Kleene, S.C., *Mathematical Logic*, London: Dover, 2002

Kockelmans, J.J.(ed.), *Contemporary European Ethics*, New York: Anchor Books, 1972

Köhler, W., *Gestalt Psychology*, New York: Liveright, 1992

Kolakowski, L., *Main Currents of Marxism*, 3 vols, Oxford: Oxford University Press, 1978

Kolakowski, L., *Positivist Philosophy*, Harmondsworth: Penguin Books, 1972

Kuhn, T., *The Structure of Scientific Revolutions*, 2nd edition, Chicago: University of Chicago Press, 1971

Kymlicka, W., *Contemporary Political Philosophy*, Oxford: Clarendon Press, 1990

Lakatos, I., "Falsification and Methodology of Scientific Research Programmes", in I. Lakatos and A. Musgrave (eds), *Criticism and the Growth of Knowledge*, Cambridge: Cambridge University Press, 1970

Lakatos, I., "Falsification and the Methodology of Scientific Research Programmes", in I. Lakatos and A. Musgrave (eds), *Criticism and the Growth of Knowledge*, Cambridge: Cambridge University Press, 1970

Laos, N., *Foundations of Cultural Diplomacy: Politics Among Cultures and the Moral Autonomy of Man*, New York: Algora Publishing, 2011

Laos, N., *The Rediscovery of Western Esotericism*, Northampton, UK: White Crane Publishing, 2012

Laos, N., *Topics in Mathematical Analysis and Differential Geometry*, London: World Scientific Publishing Co., 1998

Lavelle, L., *Traité des Valeurs: Théorie Générale de la Valeur*, Paris: PUF, 1951

Lawrence, P.R. and Lorsch, J.W., *Organization and Environment*, Cambridge, MA: Harvard University Press, 1967

Lawson, T., *Reorienting Economics*, London: Routledge, 2003

Le Senne, R., *Le Mensonge et le Caractère*, Paris: F. Alcan, 1930

Leplin, J., *Scientific Realism*, Berkeley: University of California Press, 1984

Lindbeck, A., *The Political Economy of the New Left: An Outsider's View*, New York: Harper & Row, 1971

Lipsky, M., *Street-Level Bureaucracy: The Dilemmas of Individuals in Public Services*, New York: Russell Sage Foundation, 1980

Lord, C., Ross, L. and Lepper, M., "Biased Assimilation and Attitude Polarization: The Effect of Theories on Subsequently Considered Evidence", *Journal of Personality and Social Psychology*, Vol. 37, 1979

Macpherson, C.B., *The Political Theory of Possessive Individualism*, Oxford: Oxford University Press, 1962

Mäki, U., "Some Non-Reasons for Non-Realism in Economics", in U. Mäki (ed.), *Fact and Fiction in Economics: Realism, Models and Social Construction*, Cambridge: Cambridge University Press, 2002

Marat, J.-P., "Letter to Camille Desmoulins", June 24, 1789

Marcel, G., *Man Against Mass Society*, trans. G.S. Fraser, St Augustine's Press, 2007

Marx, K., *The Capital* (edited by F. Engels), New York: International Publishers (originally published in 1894), Vol. III, Chapter 48

Maslow, A.H., "A Theory of Human Motivation", *Psychological Review*, Vol. 50, 1943

McChesney, R.W., "Making Media Democratic", *Boston Review*, Vol. 23, 1998

McConnel, C.R., *Economics*, 5th edition, New York: McGraw-Hill, 1972

Meadows, D.H. et al., *The Limits to Growth*, New York: University Books, 1972.

Mill, J., *Commerce Defended*, Gloucester: Dodo Press, 2008 (originally published in 1808)

Mill, J.S., *Essays on Some Unsettled Questions of Political Economy*, 2nd edition, London: Longmans, Green Reader & Dyer, 1874

Miller, D., *The Icarus Paradox: How Excellent Organizations Can Bring About Their Own Downfall*, New York: Harper Business, 1990

Misak, C.J.(ed.), *Pragmatism*, Calgary: University of Calgary Press, 1999

Moore, G.E., *Principia Ethica*, New York: Prometheus Books, 1988 (originally published in 1903)

Moutsopoulos, E., *He Poreia tou Pneumatos: He Axie* (The Itinerary of Spirit: Values), Athens: 1977, in Greek

Moutsopoulos, E., *Kairos et alternance: d' Empédocle à Platon*, Athènes: Académie d' Athènes, 1989

Mullen, B. and Johnson, C., *The Psychology of Consumer Behavior*, New Jersey: Lawrence Erlbaum, 1990

Mundell, R., "Notes on the History of the Mundell-Fleming Model: Keynote Speech", *Staff Papers, International Monetary Fund*, Vol. 47 (Special Issue), 2001

Musgrave, R., *Theory of Public Finance: A Study in Public Economy*, New York: McGraw-Hill, 1959

Myrdal, G., *The Political Element in the Development of Economic Theory*, London: Routledge & Kegan Paul, 1953

Neftci, S.N., "Naïve Trading Rules in Financial Markets and Wiener-Kolmogorov Prediction Theory: A Study of 'Technical Analysis'", *Journal of Business*, Vol. 64, 1991

Nicholson, M., *Causes and Consequences in International Relations: A Conceptual Study*, London: Pinter, 1996

Nonaka, I., "Creating Organizational Order Out of Chaos: Self-renewal in Japanese Firms", *California Management Review*, Vol. 30, 1988

Norris, C., *Derrida*, London: Fontana, 1987

North, D.C., *Institutions, Institutional Change and Economic Performance*, Cambridge: Cambridge University Press, 1990

Nozick, R., "Distributive Justice", in J. Westphal (ed.), *Justice*, Indianapolis: Hackett Publishing Company, 1996

Nozick, R., *Anarchy, State and Utopia*, New York: Basic Books, 1974

Oates, W., *Fiscal Federalism*, New York: Harcourt Brace Jovanovich, 1972

Obolensky, N., *Complex Adaptive Leadership: Embracing Paradox and Uncertainty*, Burlington: Gower Publishing, 2010

Okun, A.M., *The Political Economy of Prosperity*, New York: Norton, 1970, p. 130.

Orth, J.V., "Jeremy Bentham: The Common Law's Severest Critic", *American Bar Association Journal*, Vol. 68, 1982

Outhwaite, W., *Habermas: A Critical Introduction*, Cambridge: Polity, 1994

Papadimitriou, F., "Landscape Sustainability", in P. Mairota, J.B. Thornes and N. Geeson (eds), *Atlas of Mediterranean Environ-*

ments in Europe: The Desertification Context, West Sussex: John Wiley & Sons, 1998

Pascale, R.T., *Managing at the Edge: How Successful Companies Use Conflict to Stay Ahead*, London: Viking Press, 1990

Persky, J., "Retrospectives: The Ethology of Homo Economicus", *The Journal of Economic Perspectives*, Vol. 9, 1995

Pettigrew, A., *The Awaking Giant*, Oxford: Blackwell, 1985

Pigou, A.C., *The Theory of Unemployment*, New York: A.M. Kelley, 1968 (originally published in 1933

Polanyi, K., *The Great Transformation*, Boston: Beacon Press, 2001

Polinsky, A.M., "Economic Analysis as a Potentially Defective Product: A Buyer's Guide to Posner's Economic Analysis of Law", *Harvard Law Review*, Vol. 87, 1974

Popkin, S.L., *The Rational Peasant: the Political Economy of Rural Society in Vietnam*, Berkeley: University of California Press, 1979

Popper, K.R., *The Logic of Scientific Discovery*, New York: Harper & Collins, 1959

Popper, K.R., *The Logic of Scientific Discovery*, New York: Harper & Collins, 1959

Prigogine, I. and Herman, R., *Kinetic Theory and Vehicular Traffic*, New York: Elsevier, 1971

Prigogine, I. and Stengers, I., *Order out of Chaos: Man's New Dialogue with Nature*, New York: Bentam, 1984

Quine, W.V.O., "Two Dogmas of Empiricism", in W.V.O. Quine (ed.), *From a Logical Point of View*, 2nd edition, Cambridge, MA: Harvard University Press, 1961

Rawls, J., "Kantian Constructivism in Moral Theory", *Journal of Philosophy*, Vol. 77, 1980

Rawls, J., "The Basic Liberties and their Priority", in S.M. McMurrin (ed.), *The Tanner Lectures on Human Values*, Salt Lake City: University of Utah Press, 1982, Vol. III

Rawls, J., *A Theory of Justice*, Revised edition, Cambridge, Mass.: Belknap Press, 1999 (originally published in 1971)

Regan, D.H.(1972), "The Problem of Social Cost Revisited", *Journal of Law and Economics*, Vol. 15, 1972

Reynolds, C., "Deterrence", *Review of International Studies*, Vol. 15, 1989

Richardson, L.F., "Generalized Foreign Politics: A Study in Group Psychology", in O.M. Ashford, H. Charnock et al. (eds), *Collected Papers of Lewis Fry Richardson, Vol. 2: Quantitative Psychology and Studies of Conflict*, Cambridge: Cambridge University Press, 1993

Rodgers, C., "Making It Legit: New Ways of Generating Corporate Legitimacy in a Globalising World", in J. Bendell (ed.), *Terms of Endearment: Business, NGOs and Sustainable Development*, Sheffield: Greenleaf Publishing, 2000

Roll, R., "The International Crash of October 1987", *Financial Analysis Journal*, Vol. 44, 1988

Romer, P.M., "Compound Rates of Growth"; in: http://www.econlib.org/library/Enc/EconomicGrowth.html

Romer, P.M., "Endogenous Technological Change", *Journal of Political Economy*, Vol. 98, 1990

Rorty, R., *Objectivity, Relativism and Truth: Philosophical Papers*, Vol. I, Cambridge: Cambridge University Press, 1991

Rosa, J.-J., *Euro Exit: Why (and How) to Get Rid of the Monetary Union*, New York: Algora Publishing, 2012

Rosenberg, A., *Economics: Mathematical Politics or Science of Diminishing Returns?*, Chicago: University of Chicago Press, 1992

Rosenberg, A., *Microeconomic Laws: A Philosophical Analysis*, Pittsburgh: University of Pittsburgh Press, 1976

Rothman, J., *Resolving Identity-Based Conflict in Nations, Organizations, and Communities*, San Francisco, CA: Jossey-Bass Publishers, 1997

Rutherford, M., "Clarence Ayres and the Institutionalist Theory of Value", *Journal of Economic Issues*, Vol. 15, 1981

Sabine, G.H. and Thorson, T.L., *A History of Political Theory*, 4th edition, Florida: Holt, Rimehart and Winston, Inc., 1973

Sachs, J., Tornell, A. and Velasco, A., "The Mexican Peso Crisis: Sudden Death or Death Foretold?", *Journal of International Economics*, Vol. 41, 1996

Sahlins, M., *Stone Age Economics*, 2nd revised edition, London: Routledge, 2003

Samuelson, P.A. and Nordhaus, W.D., *Economics*, 14th edition, New York: McGraw-Hill, 1992

Sardar, Z. and Abrams, I., *Introducing Chaos*, Cambridge: Icon Books, 1999

Sartre, J.-P., *Being and Nothingness*, trans. H.E. Barnes, New York: Washington Square Press, 1992 (originally published in French in 1943)

Schilpp, P.A.(ed.), *The Philosophy of Karl Jaspers*, New York: Tudor Publishing Company, 1957

Schlesinger, H., Speech in Los Angeles, April 16, 1993: http://www.brugesgroup.com

Schrodt, P.A., "Adaptive Precedent-Based Logic and Rational Choice; a Comparison of Two Approaches to the Modelling of International Behavior", in U. Luterbacher and M.D. Ward (eds), *Dynamic Models of International Conflict*, Boulder: Lynne Rienner, 1985

Schwartz, P., *The New Political Economy of J.S. Mill*, London: Weidenfeld & Nicolson, 1972

Scott, D.R., "Veblen Not an Institutional Economist", *American Economic Review*, Vol. 23, 1933

Searle, J., *The Rediscovery of the Mind*, Cambridge, Mass.: MIT Press, 1992

Segal, L., *The Dream of Reality*, New York: Norton, 1986

Sellars, R.W., "The Spiritualism of Lavelle and Le Senne", *Philosophy and Phenomenological Research*, Vol. 11, 1951

Serge, V., *Les Anarchistes et l'expérience de la révolution russe*, Paris: Bibliothèque du travail, 1921

Seyhun, H.N., "Overreaction of Fundamentals: Some Lessons from Insiders' Response to the Market Crash of 1987", *Journal of Finance*, Vol. 45, 1990

Shannon, C., "A Mathematical Theory of Communication", *Bell System Technical Journal*, Vol. 27, 1948

Shleifer, A., *Inefficient Markets: An Introduction to Behavioural Finance*, Oxford: Oxford University Press, 2000

Simon, H.A., *Administrative Behavior*, New York: Macmillan, 1947

Simon, H.A., *Reason in Human Affairs*, Oxford: Basil Blackwell and Stanford: Stanford University Press, 1983

Sinclair, N., *The History of the Geometry Curriculum in the United States*, Information Age Publishing, Inc., 2008

Singer, J.W., "Democratic Values and the American Constitution Society", *Harvard Law and Policy Review Online*, September 18, 2006

Slovik, P., Fischhoff, B. and Lichtenstein, S., "Regulations of Risk: A Psychological Perspective", in R.G. Noll (ed.), *Regulatory Policy in the Social Sciences*, Berkeley: University of California Press, 1985

Smith, A., *The Theory of Moral Sentiments*, ed. D.D. Raphael and A.L. Macfie, Oxford: Oxford University Press, 1976 (originally published in 1759)

Smith, A., *The Wealth of Nations*, New York: Penguin Classics, 1986 (originally published in 1776)

Smith, S., "Positivism and Beyond", in S. Smith, K. Booth and M. Zalewski (eds), *International Theory: Positivism and Beyond*, Cambridge: Cambridge University Press, 1996

Solow, R.M., "Technical Change and the Aggregate Production Function", *Review of Economics and Statistics*, Vol. 39, 1957

Spero, J., *The Politics of International Economic Relations*, London: Allen and Unwin, and New York: St Martin's Press, 1990

Spiegelberg, H., *The Phenomenological Movement*, 3rd revised and enlarged edition, The Hague: Nijhoff, 1982

Stacey, R.D., *Strategic Management and Organizational Dynamics*, London: Pitman, 1993

Stephenson, H.W., *Forecasting Opportunity: Kairos, Production and Writing*, Lanham, Maryland: University Press of America, 2005

Strayer, J.K., *Linear Programming and Its Applications*, New York: Springer-Verlag, 1989

Ströker, E., *Husserl's Transcendental Phenomenology*, Stanford: Stanford University Press, 1993

Takahashi, M.A., Fraser, N.M. and Hipel, K.W., "A Procedure for Analyzing Hypergames", *European Journal of Operational Research*, Vol. 18, 1984

Taleb, N.N., *The Black Swan: The Impact of the Highly Improbable*, New York: Random House, 2007

Thom, R., *Mathematical Models of Morphogenesis*, trans. W.M. Brookes and D. Rand, Chichester: Ellis Horwood Ltd, 1983

Thucydides, *The Peloponnesian War*, trans. B. Jowett, Oxford: Clarendon Press, 1900 ("Funeral Oration of Pericles")

Tiebout, C., "A Pure Theory of Local Expenditures", *Journal of Political Economy*, Vol. 64, 1956

Tietmeyer, H., Speech in Berlin, September 9, 1994: http://www.brugesgroup.com

Tiles, M., *Bachelard: Science and Objectivity*, Cambridge: Cambridge University Press, 1984

Toffler, a., *Future Shock*, New York: Bantam Books, 1971

Toffler, A., *Powershift: Knowledge, Wealth and Violence at the Edge of the 21st Century*, New York: Bantam Books, 1991

Toffler, A., *The Third Wave*, London: Pan, 1981

Touraine, A., *The Post-Industrial Society*, London: Wilwood, 1974

Turing, A., "Computing Machinery and Intelligence", *Mind*, Vol. LIX, 1950

Tversky, A. and Kahneman, D., "Judgment under Uncertainty: Heuristics and Biases", *Science*, New Series, Vol. 185, 1974

United Nations, "Report of the World Commission on Environment and Development", General Assembly Resolution 42/187, December 11, 1987

van Dijk, J., *The Network Society*, 2nd edition, London: Sage, 2006

van Norden, S. and Schaller, H., "Speculative Behaviour, Regime-Switching and Stock Market Crashes", Bank of Canada Working Paper 96-13, October 1996

Varoufakis, Y., *Rational Conflict*, Oxford: Blackwell, 1991

von Glasersfeld, E., *The Construction of Knowledge*, Salinas, CA: Intersystems, 1987

von Neumann, J., *First Draft of a Report to the EDVAC*, Moore School of Engineering, University of Pennsylvania, June 30, 1945

Waldrop, M.M., *Complexity: The Emerging Science at the Edge of Order and Chaos*, London: Viking, 1992

Weaver, W., "The Mathematics of Communication", *Scientific American*, Vol. 181, 1949

Weizenbaum, J., *Computer Power and Human Reason: From Judgment to Calculation*, London: Penguin, 1984

Whitehead, A., *Science and the Modern World*, New York: Macmillan, 1944

Williams, R., *Towards 2000*, Harmondsworth: Penguin, 1985

Williamson, O.E., *Markets and Hierarchies: Analysis and Antitrust Implications*, New York: Free Press, 1975.

Winch, P., *The Idea of a Social Science and Its Relation to Philosophy*, London: Routledge, 1990

Witte, E., "Field Research on Complex Decision-Making Processes: The Phase Theorem", *International Studies of Management and Organization*, Vol. 2, 1972

Wolf, M., "Why Germany Cannot Be a Model for the Eurozone", *Financial Times*, March 30, 2010

Wolfram, S., "Computer Software in Science and Mathematics", *Scientific American*, September 1986

Woodcock, A. and Davis, M., *Catastrophe Theory*, London: Penguin Books, 1991

Zerbe, R.O., Jr, "The Problem of Social Cost in Retrospect", *Research in Law and Economics*, Vol. 2, 1980

INDEX